HIROSHIMA

Victoria Sherrow

A Timestop Book

New Discovery Books
New York

Maxwell Macmillan Canada
Toronto

Maxwell Macmillan International
New York   Oxford   Singapore   Sydney

Designer: Deborah Fillion
Cover photo: AP/Wide World Photos
All interior photos courtesy of The Bettmann Archive except p. 71, courtesy
of AP/Wide World Photos

New Discovery Books
Macmillan Publishing Company
866 Third Avenue
New York, NY 10022

Maxwell Macmillan Canada, Inc.
1200 Eglinton Avenue East
Suite 200
Don Mills, Ontario M3C 3N1

Macmillan Publishing Company is part of the Maxwell Communication Group
of Companies.

First Edition

Printed in the United States of America

10 9 8 7 6 5 4 3 2 1

Library of Congress Cataloging-in-Publication Data
Sherrow, Victoria.
    Hiroshima / by Victoria Sherrow. — 1st ed.
       p. cm.
    "A timestop book."
    Includes bibliographical references and index.
    ISBN 0-02-782467-5
    1. Hiroshima-shi (Japan)—History—Bombardment, 1945—Juvenile literature. 2.
World War, 1939–1945—Japan—Juvenile literature. 3. Atomic bomb—Juvenile literature. [1. Hiroshima-shi (Japan)—History—Bombardment, 1945. 2. World War,
1939–1945. 3. Atomic bomb.] I. Title.
D767.25.H6S495 1994
940.54'25—dc20   93-30428

Summary: An examination of the events leading up to, including, and following the drop-
ping of the first atomic bomb, on the Japanese city of Hiroshima.

0-382-24742-6 (pbk.)

**For my editor,
Henry Rasof**

Almost 12 years after the bombing of Hiroshima, another atomic bomb is tested in the Nevada desert.

CONTENTS

Smoke rises 20,000 feet above Hiroshima on August 6, 1945, after the first atomic bomb was dropped.

PROLOGUE:
A BLINDING
FLASH
OF LIGHT

Before dawn on August 6, 1945, a B-29 called the *Enola Gay* roared down the airstrip on the northern Pacific island of Tinian in the Marianas, about 1,300 miles south of Japan. Watching it lift off and soar above the ocean, U.S. military officials were relieved. They had worried that this plane, loaded with an unusual cargo and 7,600 gallons of fuel, might be too heavy to leave the ground. The *Enola Gay* was built larger and heavier than standard B-29s so that it could carry a new kind of bomb, built by some of the world's most famous scientists. The scientists had estimated that this new bomb might have the power of 20 million tons of the explosive TNT, able to kill 20,000 people or more in one blast.

Still, such a weapon had never been used in war before and nobody was certain what would happen when the *Enola*

The ground and flight crew of the Enola Gay *after the bombing mission on Hiroshima*

Gay took off that morning. If the bomb exploded during takeoff, it would destroy Tinian and everybody on it. For that reason, the bomb was not armed until the plane was in flight. So secret was the mission that some members of the crew had not been told exactly what kind of bomb they were carrying until the day of the mission itself. Through clear skies, the *Enola Gay* flew toward its destination: Japan, with whom the United States was at war.

The top secret flight of the *Enola Gay* took place during the last days of World War II, a long, bloody conflict that caused tremendous destruction and millions of deaths. America had declared war on Japan in December 1941, after the Japanese navy bombed the principal U.S. naval base, at Pearl Harbor, Hawaii. At that time, America also joined its European allies, including Great Britain and France, in fighting Japan's allies, Nazi Germany and Italy—the Axis nations. Italy joined the Allies in 1943. Germany surrendered in 1945 before the flight of the *Enola Gay*, ending the war in Europe. But Japan continued to fight the war in the Pacific.

U.S. government and military leaders thought that Japan eventually would surrender, but nobody was sure when that would happen or how many people on both sides would die in the meantime. During the spring and summer of 1945, these men debated the best way to end the war. One option was to shock the Japanese by using the newly invented atomic bomb, which was successfully tested that July. Their decision led to the August 6 flight of the *Enola Gay*.

World War II had turned into what many people called a "war of weapons." New technology led to the development of more destructive kinds of planes, missiles, tanks, guns, and bombs. Cities, including those with large civilian populations, were bombed on a larger scale than in any previous war. Scientists in other nations, including Germany and Japan, had also conducted nuclear research during the war, hoping to develop atomic weapons. But the United States had been the first to achieve this goal, through an intense, organized effort and at a cost of $2 billion. Now the *Enola Gay* was preparing to drop the most devastating weapon yet known to humankind.

The bomb had been armed, or "live," for several hours when the B-29 reached its target, Hiroshima, Japan, where there was a military base and a city and suburban population of about 380,000. At that point, the captain, Colonel Paul Tibbets, and the crew knew they were about to make history. The bomb was released over a bridge that stretched across the city's Ota River.

About 1,800 feet above Hiroshima, the bomb exploded. Below, the men, women, and children of the city were going about their usual morning activities—eating breakfast, working at their jobs or household chores, attending school, or moving about the streets. When the bomb exploded, as many as 130,000 people may have died at once. Survivors later described an incredible flash of light and extreme heat, for the bomb created temperatures thousands of times hotter than the surface of the sun. One observer tried to put into words the ghastly sights and sounds that followed:

> Within a few seconds the thousands of people in the streets and the gardens of the center of town were scorched by a wave of searing heat. Many were killed instantly, others lay writhing on the ground screaming in

agony from the intolerable pains of their burns. Everything standing upright in the way of the blast, walls, houses, factories and other buildings, was annihilated and the debris spun round in a whirling wind and was carried up into the air.[1]

While viewing the blast, a member of the *Enola Gay's* crew, Robert Lewis, wrote in the plane's log, "My God, what have we done?"[2] A Japanese journalist called Hiroshima a "zone of utter death in which nothing remained alive."[3] Many of the stunned people of Hiroshima later called it hell on earth; some could not bring themselves to speak of it at all.

The death and destruction were vast and did not end on that day. Many who did not die during the bombing or shortly thereafter suffered long-lasting effects, enduring pain, terrible scars, disabilities, and chronic health problems. The radioactivity emitted by the bomb led to radiation sickness and high rates of cancer and other diseases. Some children of survivors were born with mental and physical problems brought on by the cell damage that radiation can cause.

Three days after Hiroshima, a second atomic bomb was dropped, this time on Nagasaki, a city with steel and arms-building plants and about 200,000 people. Japan surrendered on August 14. The bombings have been credited with bringing an end to World War II and saving millions of lives.

They also have been called the worst human-made disasters in history. People still question whether atomic weapons should ever have been used. Were these weapons a remarkable scientific achievement, a necessary evil, or cruel and immoral?

Because Hiroshima was the target of the first atomic bomb, the name of this city has come to stand for the dawn of the atomic age. Likewise, Hiroshima is a symbol of international efforts for disarmament and world peace. "No More Hiroshimas," say those who believe that atomic weapons must never again be used on earth.

August 6, 1945, was a day that changed history. Atomic weapons had arrived, and there was no turning back. After World War II, newer and more destructive nuclear arms were created. An arms race destined to last for decades took place between the United States and the Soviet Union. Numerous other countries also developed atomic weapons, and the people of the world continue to live with the nuclear threat.

Like the rest of Japan, Hiroshima was rebuilt and now houses thriving industries and more than one million people. Rebuilt, too, is the relationship between America and Japan, now political allies and trading partners. The road to peace and friendship was a difficult one. Starting with Pearl Harbor, loss of life on both sides preceded a bombing that killed more than 100,000 people in a day and turned an ancient city on the Ota River into charred rubble.

CHAPTER ONE: CASTLE TOWN IN THE LAND OF THE GODS

"**M**y beautiful Hiroshima, a city of lush greenery and clear water," is how one prewar resident described her native city.[1] As the morning sun rises, crimson tinges the mountains, then glows across the seven streams that divide this delta city into six islands. These streams branch off the Ota River, which flows from the Chugoku Mountains and connects Hiroshima to the Inland Sea. The city air smells of saltwater, as the tides bring water from the sea into the freshwater streams. The semicircle of mountains shields

Hiroshima from the cold northerly winds that arise in the Japan Sea, leading to mild winters and hot summers.

Located in a bay on the southern tip of Honshu, Japan's major island, Hiroshima is well placed to be a port city. Yet the Ujina Port there was not finished until 1889. Until then, Hiroshima was a quiet, provincial town, isolated, like the rest of Japan, from most of the outside world.

In ancient times, the area that became Hiroshima was called Ashihara—"reed field"—for the dense reeds that grew on the marshy deltas along with thick groves of pine trees and graceful weeping willows. Early settlers could enjoy picturesque views of the silver-blue Inland Sea, with its thousands of small islands. Fishing villages sprang up on the coastal islands because of the abundant fish and shellfish. Clams and oysters could be found along the sandy shores, while squid, sardines, and other fish swam in the waters. The mountain valleys had fertile soil that proved suitable for growing rice and wheat.

Although Shintoism had been the official religion since ancient times, during the 6th and 7th centuries, Buddhism gained prominence and a Buddhist temple was built in Ashihara. During the 9th century, a major Shinto shrine was erected on Miyajima, an island just off the Hiroshima coast. People visited Miyajima to pray and to admire the ornate wooden shrine, painted vivid orange-red. Young men came to learn how to become Shinto monks.

Until the 9th century, Japan was ruled by a long line

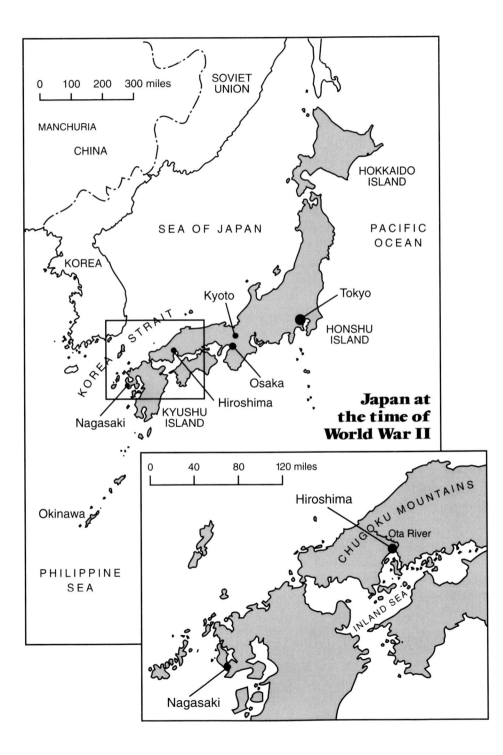

0   100   200   300 miles

SOVIET
UNION

MANCHURIA

CHINA

HOKKAIDO
ISLAND

SEA OF JAPAN

PACIFIC
OCEAN

KOREA

Kyoto

Tokyo

HONSHU
ISLAND

KOREA STRAIT

Osaka

Hiroshima

**Japan at
the time of
World War II**

Nagasaki

KYUSHU
ISLAND

Okinawa

PHILIPPINE
SEA

0   40   80   120 miles

Hiroshima

CHUGOKU MOUNTAINS

Ota River

INLAND SEA

Nagasaki

of emperors dating back to 660 B.C., when Jimmu ascended the throne. According to traditional Japanese history, the emperor was descended from gods and so was part divine and part human. This legendary history viewed Japan as the Land of the Gods, whose people shared a special and important historical destiny. From their court located in Kyoto, emperors continued to rule an expanding land area until the ninth century A.D.

At that time, court nobles assumed a larger role in governing Japan, while the emperors were assigned mostly ceremonial functions. Different imperial clans vied for power, and by the 12th century, a major civil war had broken out. Control of the Japanese government was won by a military dictatorship that stayed in power for seven centuries. Feudal rulers carried out the government policies of these rulers, called shoguns, who lived near what is now Tokyo. The emperors and their families still lived in Kyoto and had a symbolic role but no real authority.

One of these feudal lords, Motonari Mori, erected a lavish five-story wooden castle in Ashihara in 1594. He renamed the reed field Hiro-shima-jo, meaning "Broad Island Castle." Other lords and their families lived in the castle and ruled the district until 1867, the year imperial rule was restored to Japan after centuries of military dictatorship.

For centuries, the Japanese had no contact with the people of Europe or with Western ways. Their ancient culture had been influenced by neighboring China and Korea. Then, during the 1500s, sailors from Europe ventured across the Atlantic Ocean and into the Pacific Ocean to explore Asia. The first sailors to trade in Japanese ports came from Portugal in 1543. More traders followed, along with Christian missionaries, who tried to convert the Japanese to their religion.

Over time, Japanese leaders adopted an isolationist policy. Besides hoping to resist outside influences on their culture, they feared that foreigners might try to conquer Japan. After the mid-1600s, foreign traders were told to stay away, although their ships frequently passed Japan during voyages in the Pacific.

By the 1800s, the United States, a relatively new nation, found itself in a dilemma that led to a confrontation with Japan. Some American sailors were accidentally shipwrecked on Japanese soil, but Japanese leaders refused to release them. In July 1853, President Millard Fillmore sent Commodore Matthew Perry and a fleet of large, impressive ships to Tokyo Bay to demand the sailors' release. With Commodore Perry were 2,000 troops. Stories spread throughout Japan about these American sailors with their modern arms and fast battleships.

Japanese officials saw that the Americans had larger ships and were more heavily armed than their own navy. They let the American sailors go and signed a treaty with the United States in March 1854. Isolationism gradually ended as Japan also negotiated treaties with European nations.

During the next decade, 700 years of military rule ended as the Japanese imperial family regained power. In 1867, Emperor Mutsuhito ascended the throne and, following ancient tradition, gave his reign a special name, in this case Meiji—"enlightened government." Mutsuhito thought his people should learn more about the West in order to survive in a changing world. Japanese statesmen hired experts from France, Great Britain, and Holland to modernize Japan's militia and design new buildings. The 1870s saw the introduction of a new constitution based on that of France and of a system of universal education. A new form of government included a prime minister and a national legislature, but the emperor reserved certain powers for himself.

Increasing industrialization took place during Mutsuhito's reign. Although still a rural seaside town, Hiroshima, as it was now called, became more industrial. Silk making and the fishing trade grew in importance. The Ujina Port in Hiroshima was finished in 1889. The port led to an increasing military role for the city.

By the end of the 1800s, Japan was using military force to expand. It fought a war with China, the Sino-Japanese War, from 1894 to 1895. Starting in 1904, Japan fought an 18-month war against Russia. During these wars, imperial headquarters were set up in Hiroshima, and the Diet—the

Japanese lawmaking body—met there at times. The port was used to ship soldiers and supplies to the warfronts. As in every war they fought until World War II, the Japanese were victorious.

By the early 1900s, Japan had become a strong nation, with conquered territories in Manchuria, Korea, and Formosa (now Taiwan). During World War I, it fought along with the United States and the other Allied forces against Germany. When the war ended, Japan was granted some islands formerly owned by Germany. The Japanese continued to build up their navy, and by 1920, Japan was the strongest military power in Asia. It had the third-largest navy in the world, after Great Britain and the United States.

Japan met with Great Britain, the United States, and other world powers in Washington in 1922. These nations agreed to defend one another's rights in the Pacific. They also pledged to recognize the territorial rights of China. To reassure some Asian nations that feared Japan, the treaty set a limit on the size of the Japanese navy, limiting it to three ships for every four American and every five British vessels. The Japanese complained about this provision. Yet it left Japan as the sole naval power in the Pacific, which gave it an area of dominance over the other nations.

New colonies enabled Japan to grow even stronger. Japanese people settled the islands and raised more food and manufactured goods useful for the whole population. Besides homes and businesses, the Japanese built new military bases in their colonies, even though such bases were banned by a League of Nations pact Japan had signed in 1921. Hiroshima continued to house some industries that made military equipment. Its economy benefited from such industries through the years.

In December 1926, Emperor Taisho, son of former emperor Mutsuhito, died and his son Hirohito became emperor. Hirohito was a well-educated, sensitive man of 25. An avid student of marine biology, he also appreciated Western culture and had traveled in Europe a few years earlier. His reign marked the beginning of an era that he hoped would be a time of peace and progress in Japan. Like other people throughout the land, the citizens of Hiroshima paid him homage, with the words "Long life to the emperor!"

To signify his reign, Hirohito chose the name Showa, meaning "Enlightened Peace" or "Radiant Peace." Yet there was a struggle going on between the more democratic and the militaristic elements in the Japanese government. Military leaders were determined to expand Japan's territories. During the 1920s, they imported a great deal of iron, needed for steelmaking, in preparation for war.

Other economic and political events propelled Japan toward more nationalism and military aggression. The government became more chaotic in the early 1920s as different political parties sought control. A military leader, General Tanaka Giichi, leader of the Seiyukai party, took

Emperor Hirohito in 1928

firm charge as Japan's prime minister in 1927. His cabinet was made up of other militaristic-minded men.

A worldwide Great Depression began in 1929 and continued into the 1930s, hurting Japan's economy. Other countries, including the United States, imported less raw silk and other Japanese goods. Japan had no oil, rubber, or iron ore of its own and had always relied on trade to supply it with these and other raw materials.

As the economy worsened, old ideas flourished that defined Japan as a favored Land of the Gods, destined to become master of Asia. This fervor increased when China, the largest land in Asia, grew more unified under the leadership of Chiang Kai-shek. The Japanese viewed a strong China as a threat to their power and security. Japan had also worried about its neighbor Russia since the Communist Revolution that had taken place in 1917. Furthermore, there was an ongoing conflict with the United States over the limits it had imposed on Japanese immigration since the early 1900s. American laborers resented the fact that Japanese Americans would work longer hours and for less pay than American labor unions approved. Ill-treatment and anti-Japanese laws that oppressed immigrants living on the U.S. Pacific coast angered the Japanese government. Anti-American sentiments surged among people in Japan.

In 1931, a faction of the Japanese army seized northern Manchuria, part of China. Thousands of Chinese died as Japan went on to invade Shanghai and other regions in China, prompting strong criticism from nations around the world. When the League of Nations insisted that Japan withdraw from China, Japan quit the league in 1933 and formed new alliances. One was the Anti-Comintern Pact, an agreement in which Japan, Italy, and Nazi Germany agreed to jointly fight Communist uprisings in any of their countries.

Increasingly, militarism pervaded different areas of Japanese life, including toy stores. An American official wrote, "A glimpse at any toy shop, and they are numerous in Japan, will reveal the military inclinations of the people. There one can find toy soldiers, tanks, helmets, uniforms, rifles, armored motor cars, airplanes, anti-aircraft guns, howitzers, cannons, besides the usual pop guns, bugles, and drums."[2]

Boys used bamboo poles as rifles and played soldier, mimicking war activities they had heard about. Saito Mutsuo recalled that a temple near his home became an imaginary Chinese fort where he and his friends "played at being the Three Bomb Heroes of Shanghai. Three of the boys would get a large log of wood and tie it to their backs with string, to be the 'bomb,' and the rest of us would be enemy guards and so on. We were very impressed by the story of the Three Bomb Heroes. We were told that only Japanese soldiers could do something like that."[3]

In many ways, daily life in Hiroshima had not changed much up to this time. On the streets, men could be seen wearing traditional kimonos, while women bustled about, shopping at the usual stores. In spite of the Depression, people had enough to eat. Restaurants featured the oysters and other seafood for which Hiroshima was known. Tea shops sold drinks and sweets, including popular bean paste cakes shaped like maple leaves. Tourists enjoyed the beaches and visited the Miyajima shrine. Schoolchildren completed their lessons and carried a lunch usually made up of rice, salted fish, and pickled plums. Rice cakes could still be had for special occasions.

Meanwhile, the government expanded the war in China. In 1936, Japan revoked the 1922 agreement it had signed in Washington and vigorously built up its navy. Japanese troops captured Nanking in December 1937. By then, Chinese deaths numbered in the tens of thousands. Japanese soldiers committed atrocities against the Chinese that were never reported in the Japanese press.

Instead, the people were told of glorious victories and urged to support Japanese military goals. In her book *My Japan: 1930–51*, Hiroko Nakamoto recalls that during the war with China, women in Hiroshima stood on the streets sewing long white cloth sashes called *senninbaris*. Women walking by would stop to add their own red stitches to these patriotic sashes, which were then sent to soldiers to wear as belts. Rice and other foods became scarcer during the late 1930s, so children had to give up rice cakes and other refreshments they once enjoyed at school picnics. They were forbidden to wear warm coats during the winter, says Nakamoto, because, "by being cold, we were reminded of the soldiers who were fighting for our country in northern China."[4]

With the military requiring more oil and gasoline, Japanese cars began using charcoal for fuel. Rice, soy sauce, salt, sugar, charcoal, and matches were being rationed.

Instead of singing songs about nature and the seasons, children were taught patriotic verses that praised soldiers going into battle. Schools conducted marches to accompany these songs. Young people joined groups that were assigned to civic work, ration distribution, and other war chores.

During the war with China, the U.S. government had condemned Japan's actions. At one point, Japan promised to stop bombing China but did not. In 1937, a Japanese plane sank an American ship, the *Panay*, and some Americans died. But the two nations avoided a direct clash. With no natural resources of its own, Japan still needed American oil, rubber, iron, tin, copper, and nickel. And Americans were not eager to join another war, even as German aggression was pushing America's allies into a war in Europe.

By 1939, the situation on that continent was reaching a crisis. The German Nazi dictator, Adolf Hitler, had begun leading an aggressive sweep across Europe. After annexing Austria, Germany invaded Czechoslovakia and Poland in 1939, which meant war with Poland's allies, England and France. On another side of the world, Japan invaded Malaya, Singapore, and the oil-rich Dutch East Indies (now Indonesia). Japan formally joined the Axis nations of Germany and Italy in September 1940. When Japan bombed French Indochina (comprised of parts of present-day Vietnam, Cambodia, and Laos) that same year, President Franklin D. Roosevelt cut off all U.S. oil and scrap iron exports.

By 1941, Germany's air force—the *Luftwaffe*—and ground troops had overwhelmed France, Belgium, Holland, Norway, Denmark, and Luxembourg. England struggled to survive the blitz—an onslaught of German bombings—and battled German troops on land with the help of U.S. arms and supplies.

Still, America stayed out of the war, although citizens were divided over the issue. Some sharply criticized aid to European allies and expenditures to strengthen the U.S. military. Other Americans warned that Hitler would conquer all of Europe, then go on to attack other nations, including the United States. German ships sank U.S. merchant marine vessels being used to help England, but even then, the United States did not join the war.

Few Americans saw Japan as a danger. After all, it was about the size of the state of California, with far less power and fewer resources than the United States. Yet it was a direct action by the Japanese military that pulled America into the war, bringing much misery to both sides and disaster for the people of Hiroshima.

CHAPTER TWO: TOWARD TOTAL WAR

Duringthe summer of 1941, Japanese people found themselves eating more and more squid, a sea animal that, while tasty, can, like any food, become tiresome as a steady diet. Large amounts of squid were being dispensed in Japan as a main food item. A teacher explained the situation to his students this way:

> "Squid is caught in coastal waters. Why are we only getting fish from coastal waters? Because the fishing fleets aren't doing deep-sea fishing any more. And why aren't they doing deep-sea fishing any more? For one thing, because they haven't enough fuel—all the fuel is going to the military now—and

for another thing because the big boats have been requisitioned by the navy. They're being fitted with weapons and turned into gunboats. So now you know what your squid rations mean—there will be war in the Pacific soon."[1]

In 1940, Admiral Isoroku Yamamoto, a great Japanese naval planner, had commented, "Japan cannot beat America. Therefore Japan should not fight America."[2] Yamamoto had lived in Washington, D.C., for two years as part of the naval staff at the Japanese Embassy. Nonetheless, the next year he would find himself carrying out orders that required him to wage war against the U.S. navy, in what became known as the war in the Pacific.

As early as 1940, U.S. intelligence agents had gathered information that foreshadowed some kind of Japanese attack on the United States. The Army Signal Intelligence Corps (SIS) handled such work in those days. Methods of collecting information and cracking foreign codes were far less efficient in those days, but an SIS team called Magic managed to decode messages that indicated danger ahead. In December 1940, the U.S. ambassador to Japan, Joseph C. Grew, wrote to President Franklin D. Roosevelt that a confrontation was inevitable: "The principal question at issue is whether it is to our advantage to have that showdown sooner or have it later."[3]

Admiral Yamamoto had been rebuked by Japanese leaders when he continued to say that it would be dangerous to attack the United States. Emperor Hirohito, who had friends in England and other Western nations, also protested the idea, but both men were overruled. In October 1940, Hideki Tojo had become both prime minister and secretary of war. He favored aggressive military action and urged his fellow Japanese to pursue victory against their enemies at any cost. Otherwise, he said, Japan would forever lose face among other nations for giving in to their demands.

In 1941, Japan and the United States were still involved in diplomatic talks regarding Japan's aggression in Southeast Asia. Even so, Prime Minister Tojo decided to attack America. Admiral Yamamoto was told to plan the attack. As a target, he chose Pearl Harbor, America's chief naval base.

Located on the island of Oahu, Hawaii, Pearl Harbor housed the Pacific Fleet, America's best ships, and the majority of U.S. naval personnel. On any given day, six to eight battleships were anchored in the relatively shallow harbor. There were, besides, numerous destroyers, aircraft carriers, cruisers, minesweepers, and submarines. At nearby Hickam, Wheeler, and Bellows Fields were rows of army planes, while marine bombers were kept at Ewa Field. The presence of these fighter planes led many U.S. military experts to conclude that anyone thinking of attacking Pearl Harbor would decide against it, because so many aircraft were available for a counterattack.

Months of planning preceded the attack on Pearl Harbor, called Operation Hawaii. Yamamoto feared that the Japanese eventually would have to negotiate peace with the United States, because America had stronger military forces. He hoped to gain time by destroying as many U.S. ships as possible at one time.

On December 7, 1941, hundreds of Japanese pilots had an early-morning meal of rice cooked with small red beans—*sekihan*—eaten on solemn occasions, and red snapper. With it they drank a rice wine called sake. For these pilots, risking death in battle was part of their code of honor. Aware that they might die that day, they donned helmets, scarves printed with the word *Hissho* (certain victory), and the thousand-stitch belts sewn by Japanese women and worn for good luck.

At 6:20, 185 planes of the Japanese First Air Fleet took off. Another group soon followed, for a total of about 350 bombers. Japanese submarines also headed through the deep blue water for Pearl Harbor, where the Americans were unprepared for what followed. As their bombers neared the naval base, the pilots heard a Japanese song coming over a Honolulu radio station. There was no indication that military personnel on the island spotted the Japanese bombers. Radar operators had noticed unusual blips on their units but thought they were false alarms or U.S. aircraft.

The sneak attack took place just before 8:00 A.M. Hawaiian time. The hum of the Japanese Zeros (bombers)

A section of Pearl Harbor is engulfed in smoke shortly after the first strike by Japanese bombers.

became a roar as they reached the harbor. The first ship hit by a Japanese torpedo, launched by submarine, was the *Raleigh*, followed by its neighbor, the *Utah*. An attack alarm was sounded by the ship's officer, who saw that the low-flying planes bore bright red rising suns, the insignia of Japan's flag, on their fuselages and wings. Sure of victory, Japanese pilots cried out, "*Atarimashita!*—It struck!" as they shot at the groups of ships.

More than 2,000 sailors on board five American ships died in a matter of minutes. Many of them drowned when

The U.S.S. Arizona *goes down in flames.*

they were trapped inside their waterlogged ships. Others died from smoke inhalation or explosions or while trying to swim through water aflame with burning oil. Sailors tried to save burning comrades but most of the injured men died on the way to shore. Dead bodies lay scattered on the decks and on the water.

On just one ship, the *Arizona*, 1,177 men died when the million tons of gunpowder aboard exploded from the bombing. Among the casualties were the captain, crew

A rescue boat picks up one of the sailors from the West Virginia.

members, an admiral, members of the ship's band, and two sailors who were father and son.

There were 429 victims aboard the *Oklahoma*. George DeLong, a survivor, later recalled hearing the ship's mate yell, "Man your battle stations and set watertight conditions!" After more explosions, said DeLong, "The ship leaned and went over. Its masts stuck in the shallows, keeping the hull from going under. But the lights went out and the water rushed in through the air vent."[4]

U.S. soldiers in New York read about the Japanese attack on Pearl Harbor. On facing page: The December 8, 1941, front page of a New York newspaper announces the entry of the United States into World War II.

Mary Ann Ramsey, daughter of a navy commander, was 16 years old when Pearl Harbor was bombed. She and her mother hurried to shelter in a nearby basement. She remembered "the sound of exploding bombs and the whine of planes—the fragments of exploding ships and great billows of black smoke everywhere. We were gripped by shock, fear, and anger." Soon wounded people came, "some with filthy black oil covering shredded flesh. We placed them on mattresses. . . . We tried to reassure them."[5]

Pearl Harbor was in shambles, full of smoke, fire, and dead bodies. The stench of burned oil filled the air. After striking the harbor, the Japanese Zeros had gone on to bomb the planes at Hickam Field shortly after 8:00 A.M. People ran across the airfields and out of the hangars and other buildings to see what had happened, then to try to avoid

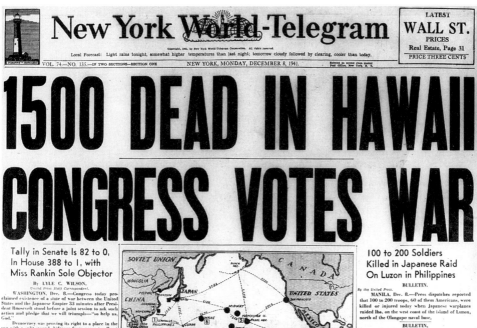

New York World-Telegram

Copyright, 1941, by New York World-Telegram Corporation. All rights reserved.

Local Forecast: Light rains tonight, somewhat higher temperatures than last night; tomorrow cloudy followed by clearing, cooler than today.

VOL. 74—NO. 135.—IN TWO SECTIONS—SECTION ONE   NEW YORK, MONDAY, DECEMBER 8, 1941.   Entered as second class matter Post Office, New York, N. Y.

LATEST
WALL ST.
PRICES
Real Estate, Page 31
PRICE THREE CENTS

1500 DEAD IN HAWAII
CONGRESS VOTES WAR

Tally in Senate Is 82 to 0, In House 388 to 1, With Miss Rankin Sole Objector

By LYLE C. WILSON.
United Press Staff Correspondent.

WASHINGTON, Dec. 8.—Congress today proclaimed existence of a state of war between the United States and the Japanese Empire 33 minutes after President Roosevelt stood before a joint session to ask such action and pledge that we will triumph—"so help us, God."

Democracy was proving its right to a place in the sun with a split-second shiftover from peace to all-out war.

The Senate acted first, adopting the resolution by a unanimous roll call vote of 82 to 0, within 21 minutes after the President had concluded his address, amid tumultuous cheering of both houses.

The House vote was 388 to 1.

The lone dissenting vote was cast by Representative Rankin (R., Mont.). It was she who in the small hours of April 6, 1917, faltered, wept and finally voted no against a similar resolution aimed at Germany.

A chorus of hisses and boos greeted her vote.

Representative Knutson (R., Minn.), who also voted against American entry into the World War in 1917, said today this motion "has no choice but to declare war on Japan."

"I do not see that we have any other choice," Mr. Knutson told reporters . . . "They declared war on us."

Miss Rankin and Mr. Knutson are the only present members of the House who voted against war in 1917.

Only Miss Rankin and Representative Hoffman (R., Mich.) remained seated when the House gave a standing ovation its response to President Roosevelt's solemn statement:

"I ask that the Congress declare that since the unprovoked and dastardly attack by Japan on Sunday, Dec. 7, a state of war has existed between the United States and the Japanese empire."

All Measures for Defense.

In a staccato of short sentences, the President told where the Japanese had hit yesterday throughout the Pacific area and how their representatives "here had at the same time been continuing deceptive and false negotiations for maintenance of peace. And, he

(Continued on Page Eleven.)

The Weather

Official United States Forecast.
New York and Metropolitan area—Light rains tonight, somewhat higher temperature than last night; tomorrow cloudy with clearing.

Connecticut—Snow, changing to occasional light rain, warmer tonight; tomorrow cloudy, followed today by rain or drizzle, colder in extreme west portion.

New Jersey—Cloudy and somewhat warmer, occasional light rains tonight; tomorrow cloudy followed by clearing, colder.

(text continues)

Highest and lowest temperatures . . .

Roosevelt's War Message To Congress

By the United Press.
WASHINGTON, Dec. 1.—The text of President Roosevelt's war Message to Congress:

TO THE CONGRESS OF THE UNITED STATES:
Yesterday, Dec. 7, 1941—a date which will live in infamy—the United States of America was suddenly and deliberately attacked by naval and air forces of the Empire of Japan.

The United States was at peace with that nation and, at the solicitation of Japan, was still in conversation with its government and its Emperor, looking toward the maintenance of peace in the Pacific.

Indeed, one hour after Japanese air squadrons had commenced bombing in Oahu, the Japanese Ambassador to the United States and his colleague delivered to the Secretary of State a formal reply to a recent American message. While this reply stated, that it seemed useless to continue the existing diplomatic negotiations, it

(Continued on Page Two.)

Britain Declares War on Japan
Becomes Ally of U. S., China and Thailand

By the Associated Press.
LONDON, Dec. 8.—Britain, like the United States under Japanese attack, declared war today on the ones with wives and children—were giving up to the boss Tokyo government without waiting for Washington first to formulate an American declaration.

Said Prime Minister Churchill:

"It only remains for the two great democracies to face their tasks with whatever strength God may give them."

At the same time Britain made allies of Thailand and Free China. Prime Minister Churchill said Commons that instructions had been forwarded to the British Embassy in Tokyo and that at 1 p. m. (7 a. m., E. S. T.) a note was

(Continued on Page Twelve.)

Axis and U. S. at War, Rome Radio Asserts

The Rome Radio said today that the Japanese declaration of war "involves in accordance with the three-power pact the existence of a state of war between the new Axis powers (Italy and Germany) and the United States." CBS heard the broadcast.

All Draft Quotas To Be Increased

By the United Press.
BOISE, Idaho, Dec. 8.—Brig. Gen. Lewis B. Hershey, National Selective Service director, said today that all state draft quotas would be increased immediately.

The Selective Service organization has been ready for immediate action for just such an eventuality, he said, and made quotas of some

(text continues)

Report Japanese Are Using Gas

● U.S. BASES
■ JAPANESE BASES

Over this vast stage the newest showdown war is being fought out today. In the Philippines (1) Japanese bombers struck twice during the day at Davao, Baguio and Fort Stotsenberg, with Japanese claiming American planes downed at Clark Field and the Japanese troops advanced on Hongkong (2), and battled the British on the beaches of Malaya (3), where Japanese bombers hit Singapore, and Thailand (4) appeared ready to yield passage to Japanese invading from the sea and Indo-China. The American Pacific Fleet steamed to battle from Pearl Harbor, in Hawaii (5), after Japanese raids aimed at battleships and killed men in Hickam Field barracks. Elsewhere the far-flung Japanese forces occupied Shanghai, seizing an American communications ship and sinking a British gunboat; laid siege to Guam, reportedly captured Wake Island (6), and raided Nauru (7).

W—World-Telegram Map

Navy Enlistment Office Swamped by Volunteers
Number Quitting Jobs to Join Is Double That of Last War

All over town today young men—and quite a few old ones with wives and children—were going up to the boss and saying "I quit!" By the hundreds, from the Bronx to Staten Island, they overran the Army, Navy and Marine recruiting offices with such gusto that the Navy had to close down for the day shortly after noon.

In response to what seemed an authorities said was a "critical" need of men, fully 1200 showed up to volunteer, besides another 500 new recruits. The navy volunteering ran more than twice as high as for the first day of war in 1917, and the whole day's recruiting was being hampered by the Navy Recruiting Office at 50 Church St. and by the time the offices were opened, there was a half-mile-long procession, too, thousands on a considerably smaller scale. There was much "mopping" of

(Continued on Page Twelve.)

100 to 200 Soldiers Killed in Japanese Raid On Luzon in Philippines

BULLETIN.
By the United Press.
MANILA. Dec. 8.—Press dispatches reported that 100 to 200 troops, 60 of them Americans, were killed or injured today when Japanese warplanes raided Iba, on the west coast of the island of Luzon, north of the Olangapo naval base.

BULLETIN.
Radio messages heard in New York at 2:10 p. m. this afternoon indicated that an air raid then was in progress over Manila. NBC's correspondent reported at 2:30 p. m. that Manila just has been bombed.

By the United Press.
WASHINGTON, Dec. 8.—Casualties on the Hawaiian island of Oahu in yesterday's Japanese air attack will amount to about 3000, including about 1500 fatalities, the White House announced today.

The White House confirmed the loss in Pearl Harbor of "one old battleship" and a destroyer, which was blown up.

Several other American ships were damaged and a large number of army and navy airplanes on Hawaiian fields were put out of commission, the White House disclosed.

It is reported at the same time that American operations against Japan were being carried out on a large scale, resulting already in the destruction of "a number of Japanese planes and submarines."

The White House statement said:

"American operations against the Japanese attacking force in the neighborhood of the Hawaiian Islands are still continuing. A number of Japanese planes and submarines have been destroyed.

"The damage caused to our forces in Oahu in yesterday's attack appears more serious than at first believed.

"In Pearl Harbor itself one old battleship has capsized and several other ships have been seriously damaged.

"One destroyer was blown up. Several other small ships were seriously hurt. Army and navy fields were bombed with the resulting destruction of several hangars. A large number of planes were put out of commission.

"A number of bombers arrived safely from San Francisco during the engagement—while it was under way. Reinforcements of planes are being rushed and repair work is under way on the ships, planes and ground facilities.

"Guam, Wake and Midway Islands and Hong Kong have been attacked. Details of these attacks are lacking.

"The total number of casualties on the island of Oahu are not yet definitely known but, in all probability, will mount to about 3000. Nearly half of these are fatalities, the others being wounded. It seems

(Continued on Page Eleven.)

World-Telegram Index

U. S., Japanese Fleets Believed in Battle

By the United Press.
HONOLULU, Dec. 8.—United States and Japanese fleets were believed fighting in mid-Pacific today after a Japanese air attack on the Hawaiian Islands.

The American fleet steamed out of Pearl Harbor naval base shortly after Japanese planes, attacking without a declaration of war or Japanese air warning, had bombed the Pearl Harbor and Honolulu City and scattered army and navy bases on Oahu Island.

Japan Claims Naval Supremacy
Four Battleships Reported Hit

TOKYO, Tuesday, Dec. 9. (Official Radio Picked Up by the Associated Press).—The Japanese asserted today .they had won naval supremacy over the United States in the Pacific, saying official or unofficial reports the being hit. Injured citizens cried out in pain. A number of people prayed. By day's end, it was found that 2,403 people had died and 1,178 were wounded. In the harbor, three ships were completely destroyed while 18 had serious damage. At the airfield, 188 aircraft were lost.

President Roosevelt was notified about the bombing shortly after it started. Roosevelt was shocked by the news, as were his cabinet members. FBI director J. Edgar Hoover asked to hear the noise of the bombs by phone before accepting the report as true.

Throughout America, people heard that the Japanese had bombed Pearl Harbor. Radio stations interrupted concerts and football games to spread the news. In New York City, a club made up of Japanese Americans sent a telegram to the president: "We the American citizens of Japanese descent in New York City and vicinity join all Americans in condemning Japan's aggressions against our country and support all measures taken for the defense of the nation."[6]

In Hawaii, newspaper headlines announced, WAR! OAHU BOMBED BY JAPANESE PLANES. Military officials in Oahu told the residents what to do in case more attacks occurred. There were 160,000 Japanese Americans living in Hawaii, and many expressed shock and regret, as well as fears that they would be accused of spying or be attacked by people seeking revenge. (Later, a U.S. army unit, the 442nd Regimental Command Team, composed of Japanese-American men from Hawaii, fought in Europe and became one of the most highly decorated units of World War II.) Being loyal to the United States, many Japanese Americans quickly offered to serve as interpreters and translators when war broke out.

Hiroko Tanamoto was 11 years old and living in Hiroshima when Japan attacked Pearl Harbor. Her family had relatives and friends living in the United States at that time, and she had heard that America was a rich and powerful nation. She later described her feelings upon hearing the news:

> One cold December morning, I came to school early. A classmate said: "Do you know we have started a war with America?" I could not believe it was the truth. I felt my heart beating very fast. I did not know what to say. . . . There was no school that day nor the next. We were told to stay at home and listen to the news on the radio. . . . The radio was a government monopoly and nothing was broadcast now but news of the war, with martial music in between. . . . Listening, I felt as if my blood were on fire, my body burning. The radio addressed us children, saying we must work hard for our country and prepare for the future. We did not know exactly what was meant.[7]

After the attack, President Roosevelt prepared a speech asking Congress for a declaration of war. The next day, he delivered a terse message that lasted six minutes and began with the words, "Yesterday, December 7, 1941, a date which will live in infamy, the United States of America was suddenly and deliberately attacked by naval and air forces of the Empire of Japan."

Within an hour, the U.S. Congress had declared war on Japan. To the European Allies, this was a tremendous event, for with U.S. forces and equipment, victory now seemed possible.

Americans expressed anger toward the Japanese as the country united to fight back. Japan and its Axis allies were seen as a threat to U.S. freedom and security. Some expressed anger at U.S. leaders that the navy had not been prepared for the attack. As rescue workers hurried to Hawaii, Navy Secretary John Knox inspected the damage and took photographs. President Roosevelt expressed outrage when he saw the pictures of charred bodies and massive damage.

On the day of the Pearl Harbor attack, the Japanese military also bombed the Philippines. By December 11, Japan controlled the area near Singapore as it continued to get control of Malaya. People in Hiroshima and elsewhere in Japan heard more tales extolling the prowess and courage of their military. A popular martial song was played over the radio:

Across the sea, corpses in the water;
Across the mountains, corpses in the field.
I shall die only for the Emperor,
I shall never look back.[8]

Throughout America, men lined up at recruiting offices
to enlist in the armed services. Individuals and families were
told to buy war bonds and start victory gardens to help the
Allied cause. People made blackout curtains and practiced
drills in homes and schools, as well as starting neighborhood
patrols. Factories increased their production dramatically.
The war ended much of the unemployment that had
plagued the United States since the Depression.

In Tokyo, Emperor Hirohito now reluctantly faced the
fact that his country was at war with the West. As he put
his seal upon the Imperial Rescript of war, the official Japanese declaration of war, he expressed his personal views by
writing, "It has been truly unavoidable and far from Our
Wishes that Our Empire has now been brought to cross
swords with America and Britain."[9]

In Hiroshima, the Eleventh Regiment set up its headquarters as the Pacific war began. The city, by 1941 the sev-
enth largest in Japan, held transport facilities, a quarantine
station, and munitions and supply depots. About 380,000
people lived in the city and surrounding suburbs.

Like other Japanese, people in Hiroshima now faced
growing shortages of foods and material things. More regu-

lations governed their everyday life. Fearful of attacks, some people tried to make their own home air-raid shelters. People were urged not to waste anything. Paper was saved and reused. Even the styles of school uniforms were changed to save cloth. Girls stopped wearing large square collars, and their skirts were made narrower. Businesspeople in Hiroshima were told to work on wartime materials and could not get raw materials for their factories unless they complied.

Young people worked in war-related activities. Children caught hordes of grasshoppers, both to protect crops and to make a protein-rich food for Japanese soldiers. They helped to make parachutes, sewed buttons on military uniforms, and worked as field hands, picking sweet potatoes and other crops. Another chore was to find scraps of tinfoil, which was made into war materials. Young women worked in silk-making factories or on farms as more men went to war. Teenagers worked in military offices and factories. Everyone got used to eating less rice and meat daily. Fruit and vegetable peels were also eaten.

Tsutsumi Ayako recalls how her patriotic attitudes were shaped in elementary school: "I began to get interested in the war effort. I really believed that Japan was the Land of the Gods and that it was absolutely essential that Japan should win the war, and I believed that I have to sacrifice myself to help Japan's victory. . . . At the time, I really did feel—that I was tremendously privileged to be Japanese."[10]

Classwork changed, too, as English classes were stopped. Girls concentrated on cooking, needlework, and drills more than on academic subjects. Sports like sack races and hurdling were replaced by stretcher races and team games like carrying buckets of water to mock fires.

Waging an intense war in the Pacific, Japan had conquered the islands of Corregidor, Singapore, and Manila. Japan was in control of the air and sea in that area by the end of 1942. The British navy had surrendered.

Eager for a victory, America sent ships to Alaska and Midway after cracking a code used by Japanese naval radio operators. During the battle of Midway in June 1942, U.S. planes bombed four Japanese aircraft carriers, gaining the first Allied victory against Japan thus far. The Japanese government continued to keep unfavorable news such as this away from the public.

Still, World War II seemed far from an end when President Roosevelt addressed the U.S. Congress in January 1943. He said, "Wars grow in size, in death, and destruction. . . . I shudder to think of what will happen to humanity . . . if this war ends in an inconclusive peace."[11]

Meanwhile, the war in the Pacific raged on. The Japanese continued to fight tenaciously, maintaining that their actions were in the interests of their country. Japanese were encouraged to think of Britons and Americans as *Kichiku Bei-Ei* (American and English Devils), while in America people repeated the angry words, "Remember Pearl Harbor."

Enrico Fermi, one of the leaders of the group of scientists that developed the atomic bomb

CHAPTER THREE: TOP SECRET

On the day Pearl Harbor was bombed, the U.S. government was already two years into a top secret scientific project that would dramatically affect the war. In October 1939, Alexander Sachs, a friend and adviser to President Roosevelt, brought him a letter signed by the world-famous physicist Albert Einstein. The letter read, in part:

> Some recent [scientific research] . . . leads me to expect that the element uranium may be turned into a new and important source of energy in the immediate future. . . . This new phenomenon would also lead to the construction of bombs, and it is conceivable . . . that extremely powerful bombs of a new type may also be constructed.[1]

The letter explained that key atomic research was being done in Germany. This news alarmed scientists, especially those like Einstein who had fled from Germany. After coming to power in 1933, Hitler's Nazi government had forbidden opposition, imposing harsh penalties on those who tried to resist their policies. New laws oppressed scientists, teachers, and professors. Jews were singled out for the worst persecution, including loss of their jobs. For that reason, a number of Jews and scientists left Germany.

After reading the letter, Roosevelt did not express much concern. Sachs urged him to take the letter quite seriously. Roosevelt then said, "Alex, what you are after is to see that the Nazis don't blow us up."[2] The president then agreed that the U.S. government should support atomic research. For that purpose, he approved initial funding of $6,000.

A long chain of scientific discoveries led up to that day in 1939 when Roosevelt read Einstein's letter. For centuries, scientists had thought that an atom was the smallest bit of matter and could not be divided or split. But in the 1890s, scientists discovered that certain elements, including uranium, were unstable and broke down. The process of disintegration of the atom's nucleus, called radioactivity, was shown to produce energy.

In 1897, a British physicist, J. J. Thomson, found that uranium emitted rays made up of fast-moving, negatively charged particles. These particles, which were smaller than atoms, were called electrons. Another British physicist,

Ernest Rutherford, found positively charged subatomic particles called protons, located inside the nucleus of the atom. It seemed that atoms were not solid and indivisible but instead were made up of smaller particles.

During the 1930s, key discoveries added more knowledge about how the atom worked. Significantly, these discoveries took place just as cataclysmic political events were building up to World War II. The British scientist James Chadwick discovered the neutron—a neutrally charged particle inside the nucleus of most atoms—in 1932. Two years later, Italian physicist Enrico Fermi bombarded the atoms of different elements with neutrons to see which elements could be made artificially radioactive. Some elements, such as radium, are naturally radioactive. During his experiments, he split the uranium atom, although he did not realize it at the time. In 1938, at the Kaiser Wilhelm Institute in Germany, Otto Hahn and Fritz Strassman bombarded uranium atoms with neutrons, creating new elements. They wrote about their experiments to former colleague Lise Meitner, a Jewish physicist who had fled from Nazi persecution. Analyzing their results, Meitner realized that atomic fission—splitting of atoms—had taken place.

Concerned, Meitner told her nephew Otto Frisch about the Hahn-Strassman experiments. Frisch was then working with the prominent Danish nuclear physicist Niels Bohr. All three scientists realized the significance of these experiments: Matter could be turned into energy. This was what Albert

Einstein had proposed in 1905 when he developed his famous equation $E = mc^2$. Einstein had realized that mass and energy are different forms or versions of the same thing. He had calculated that energy (E) is the product of mass (m) and the velocity or speed of light (c) squared (^{2}).

The binding energy—the energy needed to hold the uranium nucleus together—was released when the nucleus split. Since a great deal of energy was required to bind the uranium atom, splitting a great many uranium atoms in a chain reaction could be expected to produce a phenomenal amount of energy—energy that might be used for atomic weapons.

Niels Bohr brought news of the Hahn-Strassman experiments to America when he spoke at a meeting of 50 scientists on January 26, 1939. Some scientists had read about the experiments, which were also mentioned in a scientific journal. The news caused a stir that spread to universities and laboratories throughout America.

Among the most interested scientists was a Hungarian refugee physicist named Leo Szilard. Szilard had predicted the possibility of atomic energy five years earlier. He went on to conduct his own fission experiments in his small laboratory at Columbia University. When he succeeded in getting a small chain reaction in March 1939, Szilard worried about the implications of his discovery. He later wrote, "That night I knew the world was headed for sorrow."[3]

That March, Germany invaded Czechoslovakia. Szi-

Leo Szilard

lard and other scientists were upset, knowing that mines in Czechoslovakia held the world's richest supply of uranium. America also had large deposits of uranium, but mining the ore and purifying it would take time. The Nazis now controlled the Czechoslovak ore, while less than one ounce of metallic uranium existed in the United States at the time. The Allies should work as fast as possible, said the scientists.

What should be done? Scientists disagreed about whether atomic bombs could be built, but it seemed possible. Germany held some of the world's foremost scientific centers and researchers, so they were likely working on such weapons. As the Nazis expanded their conquest of Europe, scientists grew alarmed about what would happen if Germany got atomic bombs first.

Their concern led scientists to take political action. The result was the letter to President Roosevelt, signed by

Einstein but written chiefly by Szilard after he and fellow Hungarian scientist Edward Teller visited Einstein at his summer home on Long Island, New York. Szilard and Teller also urged Einstein to ask his friend Queen Elizabeth of Belgium to ship uranium to America from Belgium's African colony, the Belgian Congo (now Zaire), which had rich deposits of ore.

Shortly after Roosevelt read the letter and agreed to support atomic research, Germany invaded Poland and atomic research took on an even greater sense of urgency. The initial $6,000 went to Columbia University, where Enrico Fermi and his team tried to figure out how to set up and control a chain reaction involving uranium. The National Defense Research Committee was formed in 1940 to oversee research and allocate more funds, which it did to the tune of $40,000 that fall. Physicists at major research centers began working on different aspects of atomic research.

A remarkable pool of scientific talent from different ethnic backgrounds was available for these projects. One team was working diligently in Great Britain. In America, the Hungarian contingent included Szilard, Teller, and Eugene Wigner. The Italian-born physicists included Nobel Prize winner Fermi, whose wife, Laura, was Jewish, and Emilio Segrè. Among the German immigrants were Einstein and Hans Bethe.

Progress, however, was slow. Making the bomb was,

according to one author, a "hideously complex exercise."[4] After getting uranium from the Belgian Congo, scientists found that only a minute amount of natural uranium was fissionable. This minute part, an isotope called light uranium (U-235), made up just 1 percent of the ore and had to be laboriously separated from the rest of the uranium, the heavier isotope known as U-238. Scientists questioned whether there would ever be enough fissionable uranium (U-235) to build a bomb.

Then in 1940, scientists in Berkeley, California, found that uranium had an odd trait: When bombarded by high-energy subatomic particles, uranium turned briefly into a new, artificial element, neptunium. Neptunium, in turn, further changed into plutonium, another new, artificial element, which turned out to be highly fissionable.

British scientists also were making important findings. They wrote a report stating that a bomb could be built, possibly within two years. At this point, the Allies did not know how far along the Germans had come in their research. Government officials concluded that whichever side got the bomb first would win the war.

Building the atomic bomb became a top U.S. government priority. In fall 1941, the Office of Scientific Research and Development, made up of scientists and government officials, was formed to coordinate the effort. A few months later, Pearl Harbor was bombed, which brought the United States headlong into the war. The American atomic physicist Arthur Holly Compton, who had grown up a pacifist, saw a moral dilemma in the situation. But he concluded, "If atomic bombs could be made, only one plan was possible. We must get them first."[5]

Compton was at the University of Chicago overseeing various projects, including the work of the Fermi team. That group was now in Chicago working to develop a self-sustaining nuclear chain reaction, basic to the building of a bomb. By spring 1942, progress had been made toward that goal and in the methods of processing uranium and plutonium.

In the meantime, the government had appointed a national director for the bomb-building project: General Leslie R. Groves of the U.S. Army Corps of Engineers. Known for his management skills and ability to complete large tasks, Groves had majored in science at West Point and was knowledgeable about engineering and physics. He had hoped to serve overseas but was persuaded that this new assignment could lead to an Allied victory. Soon, Groves found himself in charge of an endeavor that intended to do something nobody was sure could be done, with technology that had never before been used.

Groves announced that from then on, all work pertaining to the bomb would be top secret. Use of the word *bomb* was even forbidden; scientists were told to use the word *gadget*. The code name for their undertaking was the Manhattan Project.

In fall 1942, Groves met with the brilliant theoretical physicist J. Robert Oppenheimer, a native of New York City who was then teaching in California. Groves asked him to be the scientific director of the Manhattan Project.

December 2, 1942, marked a turning point in the Manhattan Project. Fermi's team tested an atomic furnace, or pile, in a squash court under the stands of a former football stadium at the University of Chicago. The 500-ton pile consisted of tiers of black graphite bricks containing lumps of uranium. There were 40,000 bricks. The pile was tested with

A painting portrays Fermi and his team testing an atomic furnace at the University of Chicago.

trepidation, for the scientists were not sure they could control the atomic reaction once it began.

As the experiment progressed, Fermi smiled and said, "The reaction is self-sustaining."[6] He allowed the reaction to last 28 minutes. Cadmium rods were then placed into the pile to stop the chain reaction: The cadmium absorbed the neutrons generated by the fission of uranium. As the scientists watched, they realized they had harnessed nuclear power. One day, that power would be used for peacetime energy, but on this day it was welcomed as another step toward building military weapons.

Work on the bomb now proceeded with more confidence. At Oak Ridge, Tennessee, General Groves bought land for a large plant that would separate U-235 from uranium ore. In Hanford, Washington, a plant began producing plutonium. Other university laboratories and factories produced tools and materials needed for the Manhattan Project. Security was tight at all these places. Most of the workers did not know exactly what they were working on. People who held key posts first had to have a security clearance from the Federal Bureau of Investigation.

In summer 1942, Los Alamos, New Mexico, was chosen as the site where scientists would gather to work on the bomb together. Oppenheimer had suggested the area to Groves because of its isolated location and warm climate.

At that time, the U.S. military had still not fully recovered from the 1941 attack on Pearl Harbor. Japanese military power reached a new high in 1942 as Japanese forces conquered the Philippines, where many American and Filipino soldiers died in battle. Between 7,000 and 10,000 soldiers died or were executed during what became known as the Bataan Death March. After capturing the island of Corregidor on May 6, the Japanese had marched 11,000 prisoners north to Bataan Peninsula. Stories about the death march increased American animosity toward Japan.

In December 1942, army officials arranged to buy 54,000 acres in and around Los Alamos. The following spring, bulldozers arrived to excavate the land, and thousands of workers began building homes and labs for the scientists, the military personnel, and their families. The Los Alamos facility was surrounded by barbed wire, and Groves enforced strict military regulations.

Soon scientists began to arrive. At that time, the goal was still to beat Germany to the bomb. "We were told day in and day out that it was our duty to catch up with the Germans," said one Los Alamos scientist.[7] Hearing about the progress at Los Alamos in the months that followed, Roosevelt often told close advisers that this new weapon would save many American lives.

Working in their desert laboratories, the scientists, technicians, and support staff at Los Alamos still faced many problems as they worked to construct a working bomb. During long days and nights and with much trial and error, they tackled these problems, one by one. By 1944, Oppenheimer predicted that they might have a bomb sometime in the next year. General Groves frequently pointed out what was at stake. If their effort failed, Oppenheimer's scientific reputation would suffer and he himself would be called before a congressional investigative committee to explain why the nation had spent $2 billion for nothing.

Yet as the Manhattan Project moved steadily toward its goal, Allied troops in Europe were making headway against Germany, the original target of the bomb. The war in the Pacific raged on, however, with no end in sight.

CHAPTER FOUR: THE TIDE TURNS

During 1942 and 1943, many battles were fought between the Japanese and the Allies (including Americans, Australians, New Zealanders, and Filipinos), from one island to another in the jungles of the Pacific. The Allies hoped to reclaim the Philippines, which the Japanese had held since 1942.

In October 1944, General Douglas MacArthur, supreme commander of the Allied forces in the Southwest Pacific, led his troops onto the beach on the island of Leyte. This became known as the A-Day landing, the start of the campaign to liberate the Philippines. Two years earlier, after MacArthur had escaped to Australia during the Japanese invasion, he had uttered the now-famous words, "I shall

General Douglas MacArthur lands at Leyte on A-Day.

return." Stepping up to a mobile microphone that October day, MacArthur said, "People of the Philippines, I have returned."[1]

As the two sides battled for these islands, the Japanese military showed no signs of giving up. The month of A-Day, there was an attack by a Japanese naval suicide squadron, whose pilots were called kamikazes. These pilots faced certain death as they aimed their planes toward enemy targets.

Other kamikaze attacks followed. Individual Japanese soldiers who were left stranded on islands fought on alone rather than surrender. Americans were surprised at how willing the Japanese were to sacrifice their lives rather than admit defeat in battle. Their military code embodied strong cultural principles, including the idea that death was more honorable than surrender or defeat, which meant disgrace.

In Hiroshima, people knew that Allied air raids were taking place in cities across the country. Some refugees from these stricken places moved to Hiroshima. When would their own city be bombed? they wondered. Rumors spread. One was that Hiroshima was being spared because the U.S. president had relatives living in the city; another held that the Allies were protecting the area so they could settle there after the war, if they won.

Even so, people prepared for air raids. Crews tore down old, closely spaced wooden buildings that would burn rapidly. Workers widened the streets. People practiced drills, hurrying into air-raid shelters where water was stored. Citizens were ordered to wear air-raid hats or cloth hoods when outdoors and to carry small bags of medicine around with them at all times.

The Japanese government continued to say that their strong military was defeating the Allies. By late 1944, patriotism was still strong, but more Japanese expressed skepticism. Some young men who did not believe in the war tried to avoid being drafted by pretending to have tuberculosis, a lung disease that was widespread in Japan. Others tried to fail their physical examinations by not eating or by drinking huge quantities of soy sauce so they would seem ill.

Among the jokes circulating in the country were these: Question: What things have multiplied since the war broke out? Answer: Laws, paper money, music without songs, and lice. Question: What things have diminished? Answer: Commodities, food, and kindness.

Food grew more scarce. Japan had not produced enough food for all its people since the 1800s and had been relying upon imports from various countries to supply the rest. By now, people were used to going without treats, such as the traditional herring's roe and chestnut sweets for New Year or rice cakes at parties. By spring 1945, about three-fourths of Japan's merchant ships had been destroyed and hunger became widespread. People got food however they could. Some fortunate city residents had rural family or friends who gave them produce, such as sweet potatoes. Many meals consisted entirely of that vegetable.

Children got used to taking the same lunch to school each day. Called a Japanese Flag, it consisted of a bowl of grain with a red pickled plum in the middle. Rice was a luxury, so having too much white rice and not enough wheat or barley was considered unpatriotic.

People had to pay extravagant prices on the black market to get sugar, eggs, and sake, also considered luxuries. Black market prices were about 20 times the prewar cost, and few citizens could afford that. Many Japanese heard that government officials still got these items, often serving them at lavish parties. That caused resentment, especially when, in 1945, many Japanese were going to bed hungry.

In May 1945, the Second General Army of Japan made Hiroshima its headquarters. This division was in charge of defending western Japan in case of an Allied invasion. As the army moved into Hiroshima Castle, citizens worried that their city would now be viewed as a military target and be bombed. Besides the factories that made war materials, there was a military airstrip in the city.

New precautions against air raids and possible invasion were taken that spring. Many middle-school children helped to lay out fire prevention belts in Hiroshima. These lanes were intended to stop the spread of fires if the city were bombed.

During those months, Hiroko Nakamoto was attending high school and working in a factory. She recalls her thoughts at that time:

> We heard only good news of Japan and we believed it. One day a college girl who also worked in the factory said, "I don't believe we are being told the truth. I don't think the war is going well for Japan." We hated her. She lied. Was she pro-Western? Should we report her? No loyal Japanese would say such

things about our country. Thus it was a great
shock to us when the newspapers and radio
informed us that the war was moving closer
and we Japanese must be prepared for a fight
on our own territory. . . . The history of our
country went back more than two thousand
years. In all that time Japan had never been
invaded. We had been taught that it never
could be. Our country was protected by the
gods.[2]

Although springtime had brought warm weather and
the usual beauty of nature—blooming peach and cherry
trees, budding willows, nesting swallows—people felt tired,
hungry, and worried. They did not go boating as usual or
enjoy the customary strolls past the moat around Hiroshima
Castle, with its profusion of water lilies, or alongside the
banks of the Motoyasu River. Near the river was the most
remarkable building in Hiroshima, the domed Industry Promotion Hall, designed in 1915 by a Czech architect, Jan
Letzel. Its elaborate lighting system stayed off that spring.
Also unlit were the many riverside restaurants that had held
farewell parties for soldiers during the war. Blackouts were
enforced.

On May 4, the Japanese were shocked to hear that
Berlin, devastated by bombings, had fallen. Italy had already
surrendered to the Allies, in 1943. But Japan's prime min-

ister made a radio speech that day, saying, "I am resolved to sacrifice everything in order to continue the war. I fervently hope . . . that you, like your brothers at the front fighting for the homeland, will now gird up your loins, ready to give up your lives for your country."[3] Three days later came the news that Nazi Germany had surrendered.

Daily life in Hiroshima was grim, with worse food shortages than ever. There was no bean paste, soy sauce, vinegar, oil, sugar, or salt—none of the ordinary staples that people had used for daily cooking before the war. Even bamboo shoots and radishes were scarce. Many people spent most of the 300 yen that was a typical month's pay on food. Dinner might be boiled soybeans, a bit of rice mixed with barley or wheat, a sweet potato, or just potato stems made into soup. Some people survived by eating acorns they found growing wild.

Of that summer, Koichi Kido, Japan's Lord Keeper of the Privy Seal, later wrote: "The weather . . . was especially bad in 1945. Consequently, the rice crop forecasts were extremely bad. Everything became scarce. The food situation was gradually becoming worse and worse. Under such conditions even the soldiers had not too much to eat. There was nothing in Japan. Even we in the Imperial Household . . . had only two sweet potatoes for lunch." Kido feared that during the coming winter of 1945–1946, "tens of millions of people" would die "a dog's death from hunger and exposure."[4]

The Japanese knew that with the war in Europe won, the Allies could now put all their effort into the Pacific front. That war had cost the United States much money, many resources, and thousands of lives. The three-month-long battle for Okinawa that year had resulted in nearly 13,000 Allied deaths and 40,000 wounded. The mood of Americans at this time was one of anger and bitterness toward Japan. Japanese people were portrayed on posters and in newspaper cartoons as brutal enemies who would never give up.

Likewise, the Japanese felt bitter toward the Allies for their own suffering. During 1945, about 13 million Japanese on various Pacific islands became homeless as a result of battles and bombings. A naval blockade kept food, oil, and fuel from reaching Japanese-controlled ports in China, Korea, and Manchuria.

Nonetheless, the military rulers of Japan did not surrender. Some members of the government suggested that Japan look for a way to negotiate an end to the war, but they were outvoted. The most militant officials insisted that if Japan were to surrender, the United States would remove the emperor and put him on trial as a war criminal. They predicted that America would force a new government on Japan and even enslave the people. Therefore, said these men, Japan must continue to fight.

Toward that end, 28 million women, children, and elderly men were told they were now a People's Volunteer

The city of Tokyo lies in ruins after an air raid.

Army. They should be prepared to fight with knives and bamboo spears if the Allies invaded Japan. Soldiers were expected to pilot suicide boats and planes to attack Americans who tried to land on Japanese shores.

Air strikes continued on Japan, including a devastating bombing on Tokyo. Afterward, Emperor Hirohito, who had stayed safe in an underground shelter during the shelling, inspected the damage and was deeply upset by the death and destruction. The Allied B-29 Superfortresses commanded by General Curtis Le May moved on to other cities. Although Japan was being turned into what its foreign minister, Mamoru Shigemitsu, called a "furnace," he wrote that people remained loyal to the cause: "If the Emperor ordered it, they would leap into the flames."[5] Unknown to the Japanese, events on the other side of the world were leading up to more tragedy in the near future.

CHAPTER FIVE:
A WARNING TO SURRENDER

In April 1945, President Franklin D. Roosevelt died, and his vice president, Harry S Truman, suddenly became the nation's leader. Truman faced some of the most difficult decisions that had ever confronted a world leader. Immediately after being sworn in, he met with his cabinet. Secretary of War Henry L. Stimson remained in the room after the others had left. Truman later wrote:

> He asked to speak with me about a most urgent matter. Stimson told me that he wanted me to know about an immense project that was under way—a project looking toward the development of a new explosive of almost unbelievable destructive power. That was all he felt free to say at the time,

Harry S Truman is sworn in as president after the death of Franklin D. Roosevelt.

and his statement left me puzzled. It was the first bit of information that had come to me about the atomic bomb, but he gave me no details. It was not until the next day that I was told enough to give me some understanding of the almost incredible developments that were under way and the awful power that might soon be placed in our hands.[1]

At this point, it was clear that the war in Europe was ending, but there was still the question of when Japan would surrender. Truman asked Stimson to assemble a group of expert advisers, both scientists and military officials, who could make recommendations to him about the atomic bomb. Among the scientists were J. Robert Oppenheimer, Arthur Compton, Enrico Fermi, Ernest Lawrence, and Vannevar Bush, director of the Office of Scientific Research and Development. General Groves and General George C. Marshall, the army chief of staff, were among the military advisers. Together, these men agonized over whether to use the bomb, and if so, where and when.

One option was to hold a nonmilitary demonstration of the bomb that would persuade Japan to surrender. But this plan posed problems. The bomb might not work during the demonstration, which might encourage the Japanese to keep fighting. Or, if forewarned, the Japanese might shoot down the plane holding the bomb. They might also think it was a trick, not a real test. Compton later wrote, "Though the possibility of a demonstration that would not destroy human lives was attractive, no one could suggest a way in which it could be made so convincing that it would be likely to stop the War."[2]

The continuation of the war meant more loss of life, a strong concern of the whole panel. Groves felt that proceeding with the bombing would save lives in the long run. He later wrote, "After all, great numbers of our boys were dying every day."[3] Truman was told that between 500,000 and a million Americans would die if an invasion were needed to end the war. Several million Japanese, mostly civilians, also would perish. Even so, General Marshall and General MacArthur did not think the bomb was necessary to win the war.

Some historians conclude that the cost of the bomb— $2 billion—also influenced its use. What had all the money and effort been for if not to end the war faster?

In addition, Truman and other Western leaders were worried about what the Soviet Union, under Joseph Stalin, intended to do after the war. They feared Stalin might invade Manchuria and countries in Eastern Europe. Oppenheimer later said, "We thought the two overriding considerations were the saving of lives in the war and the effect of our actions on . . . the strength and the stability of the postwar world. We did say that we did not think exploding one of these things over a desert was likely to be very impressive."[4]

Scientists not in the advisory group also debated the use of the bomb. A number of them, including Leo Szilard and others at the University of Chicago, adamantly opposed its use. Einstein had written a letter to Roosevelt warning about the use of the bomb, but Roosevelt died before he read it.

While some military leaders thought the bomb was not needed, others viewed it as the only way to shock Japan into surrendering. Why should American troops invade the country, they asked, when there was now a way to stop the war sooner? Anger over Pearl Harbor, the treatment of prisoners of war, and the Bataan Death March may have played a role in the final decision. And some military leaders feared that Japan would not give up. Japanese soldiers had fought zealously and seemed to prefer death to surrender.

On June 1, the committee gave its report. Truman recalled:

> It was their recommendation that the bomb be used against the enemy as soon as it could be done. They recommended further that it should be used without specific warning and against a target that would clearly show its devastating strength. . . . The final decision of where and when to use the atomic bomb was up to me. Let there be no mistake about it, I regarded the bomb as a military weapon and never had any doubt that it should be used. . . . In deciding to use this bomb I wanted to make sure it would be used as a weapon of war in the manner prescribed by the laws of war. That meant that I wanted it dropped on a military target. I had told Stimson that the bomb should be dropped as nearly as possible upon a war production center of prime military importance.[5]

Truman and others said that Japan should have a chance to surrender before the bomb was used. He also thought the emperor should be permitted to stay, if that was the only barrier to a surrender. In July, he prepared to meet with Soviet leader Joseph Stalin and British Prime Minister Winston Churchill, at an important conference at Potsdam, Germany. Truman worked on the wording of a document that would ask for Japan's surrender.

As the president headed by ship toward Europe, he received word that an atomic bomb had been successfully tested in the New Mexico desert. On July 16, 1945, a plutonium bomb had exploded with a roar over Alamogordo, an isolated area about 200 miles south of Los Alamos that was owned by the army. A huge fire mass of glaring white light rose up, then hit the earth and began spiraling toward the sky, turning weird shades of green, orange, and purple. Soon the desert sands were caught in the rising heat and formed a mushroom-shaped cloud that soared thousands of feet high. All animals and plants within a mile died.

Wearing special protective goggles, the Los Alamos staff had watched it in awe. Oppenheimer later remembered:

> We waited until the blast had passed, walked out of the shelter and then it was extremely solemn. We knew the world would not be the same. A few people laughed, a few people cried. I remembered the line from the

A mushroom cloud rises after the first atomic bomb test, at Alamogordo, New Mexico.

J. Robert Oppenheimer (left) and Major General Leslie R. Groves (right) look over the twisted remains of the steel tower on which the first atomic bomb hung when it was exploded.

Hindu scripture, the Bhagavad Gita: Vishnu is trying to persuade the Prince that he should do his duty and to impress him takes on his multi-armed form and says, "Now I am become death, destroyer of worlds." I suppose we all thought that one way or another. There was a great deal of solemn talk that this was the end of the great wars of the century.[6]

When Truman arrived for the meeting of the "Big Three"—Truman, Churchill, and Stalin—on July 17, he knew the bomb was tested and ready. Secretary Stimson had sent him a carefully coded telegram informing him of the Alamogordo test, called Trinity. In his memoirs, he wrote, "The most secret and the most daring enterprise of the war had succeeded. We were now in possession of a weapon that would not only revolutionize war but could alter the course of history and civilization."[7]

The Potsdam leaders decided that Japan must surren-

(From left to right) *Winston Churchill, Harry S Truman, and Joseph Stalin at the Potsdam Conference*

der—dismantle its military, accept occupation by Allied forces, and conduct war crime trials. The Potsdam Declaration stated: "We call upon the government of Japan to proclaim now the unconditional surrender of all Japanese armed forces and to provide proper and adequate assurances of their good faith in such action. The alternative for Japan is prompt and utter destruction."[8]

In Japan, leaders discussed the Potsdam Declaration. Emperor Hirohito favored surrender, yet by custom he was expected to stay out of political decisions. Those leaders who wanted to negotiate with the Allies were again outvoted. On July 28, Radio Tokyo announced that the nation would continue to fight.

Hearing this, the American military began choosing the city that would be the target of the bomb. The advisory committee had suggested that it be a military installation or war plant near many buildings. By destroying many buildings, they hoped to create a strong psychological effect that would lead to surrender. Groves thought the city should be "big enough so the effects of the bomb would not run out."[9] To make the impact of this bomb clear, the city should be one as yet undamaged by bombs.

Four cities were listed as possible targets: Kokura, Niigata, Hiroshima, and Kyoto. Stimson insisted on removing Kyoto from the list, since it was a city he had visited and admired for its cultural and religious significance. He warned that Japan would never forgive the United States for bombing Kyoto, a revered shrine. The city of Nagasaki took its place on the list.

The time for surrender was running out. Truman had authorized the bomb to be dropped after August 3 unless Japan changed its mind before that day. All was ready on the island of Tinian, part of the Mariana chain in the Northern Pacific, where the *Enola Gay* and its crew awaited instructions.

In Hiroshima, people struggled to survive and got used to the frequent air-raid sirens that were sounded each time an Allied plane flew overhead. Hiroko Nakamoto later wrote: "At night now we seldom slept. It was summer and very hot. At home our air-raid shelter was stifling and full of mosquitoes that bit us mercilessly. . . . With the factory, the August heat, and the air raids, at night, I, like almost everyone else in Hiroshima, was tired, very tired, all the time."[10]

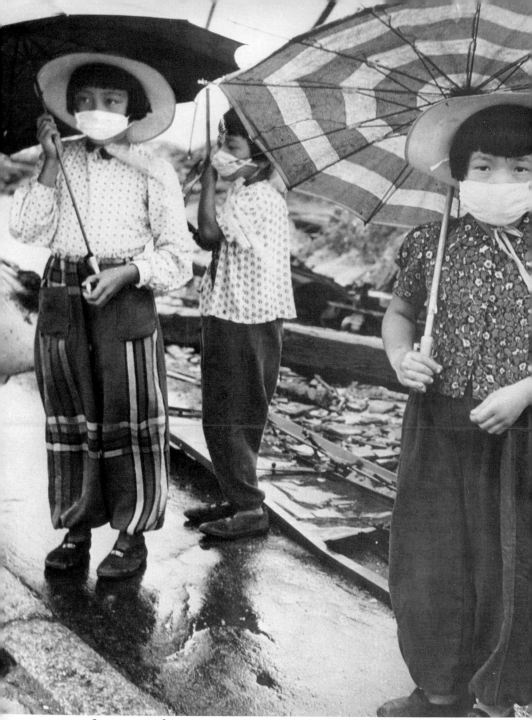

Japanese girls wear protective masks and carry umbrellas to shield themselves after the bombing of Hiroshima.

CHAPTER SIX: DAY OF FIRE AND BLACK RAIN

On August 6, 1945, an air-raid siren pierced the morning silence at 7:09 in Hiroshima. Soon afterward, the American B-29s that had prompted the warning flew away from the city. Some of the 300,000 people in Hiroshima had not gone to their designated safe areas anyway; such sirens had never meant real danger before. When the all-clear signal sounded at 7:31 A.M., those who had sought shelter resumed their daily activities without much concern.

August 6 was a hot day, with a clear blue sky. By 8:00 A.M., many people were at work or were walking, bicycling, or riding on streetcars throughout the city. Others were also doing ordinary things—cooking, eating breakfast, attending school, writing a letter, shopping, hanging clothes out to dry, reading the newspaper. Teenagers from the All-Girls Hiroshima Commercial High School had been sent to the center of Hiroshima to clear the streets of stones and wood from demolished houses. Soldiers were on duty at their posts or at the port. Many of the 40,000 men based at Hiroshima Castle were in the yard doing morning calisthenics. Twenty-three American prisoners of war were being kept at the castle, and one was being walked, blindfold, that morning.

The summer sun sparkled across the Ota River as another B-29, the *Enola Gay*, with its four-ton cargo, neared the Aioi Bridge. Many people looked up as the silver plane, which the Japanese nicknamed B-san, or Mr. B., appeared overhead. It was accompanied by two other B-29s, one carrying photographic equipment. As it released its uranium bomb 1,850 feet over the center of Hiroshima, there was a blinding flash of light. Some people also heard the boom of an explosion, but others recall only an intense bright orange or white light, as if thousands of lightning bolts were streaking across the sky at the same time. Then came a burst of tremendous heat. An eerie, multicolored dust cloud rose above the city. The shock waves that followed the explosion were so strong that large buildings collapsed and people felt themselves hurled across rooms or into the air. The time was 8:16 A.M.

The *Enola Gay*'s crew also felt intense shock waves. The gigantic mushroom cloud—like "a mass of bubbling molasses," said crew member Bob Beser—spread across the sky, blocking out the ground. Another crew member recalled, "Where we had seen a clear city two minutes before we could now no longer see the city."[1] Later, the power of the bomb was estimated to be as great as 20 million tons of TNT—20,000 times more destructive than a regular bomb.

The heat reached a land temperature of 5,400°F, twice the temperature needed to melt iron. Heat waves traveled at speeds of 1,200 feet per second within a 300-yard radius of the hypocenter (the point on the ground directly below the place where the bomb exploded). According to author Roger Rosenblatt, these incredible, fast-moving heat waves "roasted everything within a half-mile of the bridge, turning humans into charred, steaming balls of flesh."[2] The force of the explosion blew some victims' bodies to pieces, while numerous others were struck by flying bits of glass, wood, and other broken objects. At one school, 150 first graders were outdoors when the bomb exploded, and all of them died.

As clouds of smoke and dust gathered, Hiroshima became strangely dark. Then came a rash of fires, as flames spread throughout the city. The rubble that had once been Hiroshima turned to ashes. The remains of thousands of buildings lay smoldering. People who had not died at once now burned to death unless they were able to escape from the fires. Some remained trapped or unconscious inside buildings.

A group of eighth-grade girls were sitting near a Buddhist temple when the bomb exploded. A heavy fence fell on them. Trapped, they began choking from the heavy smoke. Yet in their suffering, they began to sing the national anthem, "Kimi ga yo." As they died, the girls kept singing. One of them managed to find a crack in the fence and made her way out, arriving some time later at the Red Cross Hospital.[3]

Those able to run felt a sizzling heat under their feet as they fled across the hot pavement. The crackling noise of the fires and the smells of burning buildings and burned flesh filled the air. Survivors felt a tremendous thirst and longed to cool their painful burns somehow. Many headed for water tanks or one of the rivers.

An 18-year-old schoolteacher, Katsuko Horibe, tried to lead some children to water but found the Motoyasu River covered with flaming pieces of wood and floating, swollen bodies. Shouts of "Mother! Mother!" and "This is hell on earth!" filled the air.[4] Some bridges, including the Aioi, were still standing, and people tried to cross them. Katsuko saw people so badly burned that their facial features seemed to have melted. In some cases, it was not possible to tell men from women, a person's front from his or her back.

Looking at their fellow survivors, people wondered

An Allied news correspondent surveys the damage done to Hiroshima by the bomb blast.

if they, too, had such swollen, blackened skin. Had their hair turned white or was it frizzled and standing on end? Blood and pus poured from open wounds, with some cuts so deep they exposed people's bones. Faces were missing eyelids, eyebrows, eyes, ears, noses, lips. Many people had chunks of torn skin hanging down their necks, arms, and legs. They walked with their arms held out from their bodies to keep these painful raw areas from touching anything. Clothing had been ripped from bodies or shredded, so most people were almost naked. Here and there lay piles of bodies where people had collapsed, too weary or injured to move anymore.

A high-school girl named Taeko Makamae was working at the Central Telephone Exchange that day. When the building collapsed, many of her coworkers died, but Taeko managed to get out. As she fled through the burning streets, she saw a boy about age ten begging his six-year-old sister, "Mako! Mako! Please don't die." But the little girl died as her brother wept and held her in his arms.[5]

Taeko had deep wounds on her face and left eye. With no oil or medicine to put on her wounds, someone in the crowd rubbed them with cigarette tobacco. Around her, some survivors cried out, "Kill me! Please kill me!"[6]

Those victims who made their way to the rivers found streams full of limp fish and floating bodies, some dead, some barely alive. Many people did not have the strength to swim across or stay afloat, once they were in the water. People lay on the riverbanks, moaning in pain or dead or unconscious.

The afternoon of the bomb, the sky suddenly darkened again and the air grew chilly. Rain began to fall from purple clouds in the sky, but this was black rain, unlike anything people had seen before. For several minutes, the large black drops fell, making splotches that stained skin and clothing. Water did not wash the spots away.

Two citizens of Hiroshima walk on a road flanked by piles of rubble.

Thirteen-year-old Yoshitaka Kawamoto was at school when the bomb exploded. That day, as always, he had risen at six o'clock to get ready, then had taken a train from his fishing village, Ono, into the city. Arriving at 7:45, he had joined his class in bowing to the emperor's picture and reciting the rules of conduct. Shortly afterward, one of his classmates called out, "Look! A B-29!" After seeing a flash of light, Yoshitaka fell to the floor, unconscious.

He awoke in a dark room strewn with debris. Most of his classmates, including his best friend, were dead. Those who were alive were crying out in pain and calling for their mothers. Through a hole in the roof, he saw swirling black-and-pink clouds. Outside, Yoshitaka made his way through the flames and smoke and around the fallen utility poles, wires, and other debris. Around him, survivors walked slowly, staring straight ahead or looking down, as if in a daze. Exhausted and feeling sick, he often stumbled along the way. Finally, he fainted.

He awoke in a warehouse where survivors were receiving first aid. A soldier removed a chunk of wood from his arm and gave him some ice to relieve his great thirst. Yoshitaka discovered that a few hours earlier, he had been placed on a pile of dead bodies that were about to be cremated when a soldier saw he was alive. From the warehouse, he was moved again. Hot with fever, his eyes and lips swollen, he lay in great pain. A doctor told him his injured arm should be cut off, but they managed to save it. On August 11, Yoshitaka's mother found him. That day, he wept for the first time since the bombing.[7]

Hatsuyo Nakamura, a tailor's widow, and her three children, ages ten, eight, and five, were at home when the bomb fell. She was cooking rice while the children sat eating peanuts. Then came a white flash, whiter than anything she had ever seen. She felt herself being lifted into the air, then landing amid the fallen timbers and tiles of the house. After freeing herself and her trapped children, she grabbed her one valuable possession, a sewing machine, and put it in a water tank. She led the children away from the fires to a park. In the streets came cries of, "*Tasukete!*—Help!" and "*Itai!*—It hurts!" Her children asked, "Why is it night already? Why did our house fall down?"[8] Along with about 50 others, they received care at a Jesuit chapel.

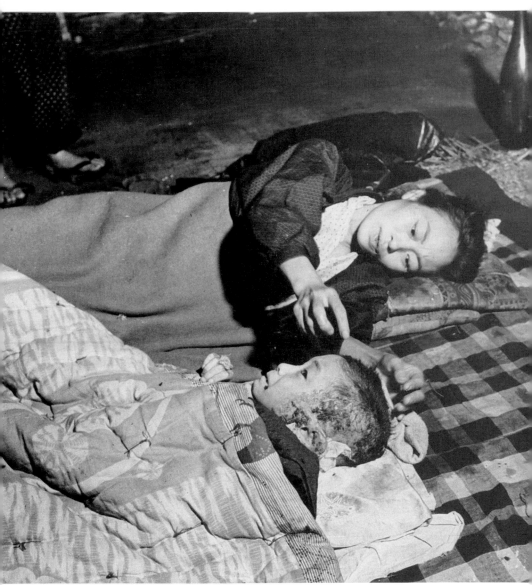

A mother tends to her burned son after the Hiroshima attack.

Mrs. Nakamura found out that her oldest son, Hideo, had burned to death in a factory. After going to a nearby town to see relatives, Mrs. Nakamura felt she had to go back to Hiroshima to find out what had happened to the rest of her family. Her mother, brother, and older sister were all dead. Many people returned to Hiroshima the evening of the bombing to look for loved ones.

Looking around after the fire, people saw that their city had virtually disappeared. There were no trees, plants, or grass. Ninety percent of the city had been destroyed, including Hiroshima Castle and 70,000 other buildings. The shells of some thick concrete buildings and the dome of the Industry Promotion Hall were about all that was left.

Satoshi Nakamura, a reporter for a news agency, telephoned his bureau chief to describe the bombing, estimating 170,000 dead. The chief argued with him, saying he must be exaggerating the extent of the damage and the number of deaths. In the days after the bombing, the Japanese were not told how badly Hiroshima had been hit. Although American newspapers contained headlines that said, ATOMIC BOMB DROPS ON JAPAN, the Japanese press called the weapons "special bombs" or "new type bombs."

Japanese physicists were sent to Hiroshima, and some concluded that the bomb had indeed been atomic. On August 6, navy minister Admiral Yonai wrote a top secret memo that read, "Hiroshima destroyed by atomic weapon. This war is lost."[9]

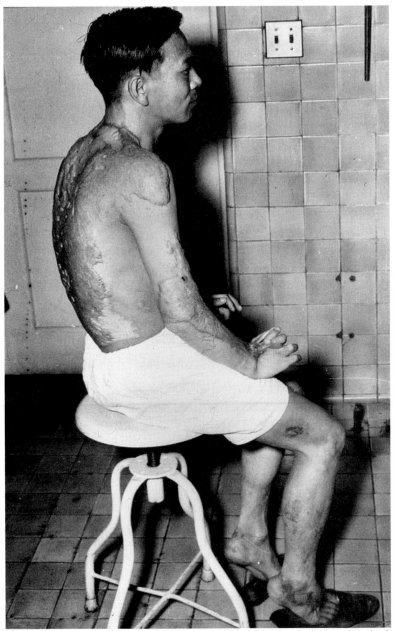

One of the many victims of the Hiroshima bombing shows the thick keloid scars that covered his body two years after the explosion.

On August 7, the day after the bombing, the East Drill Ground was being used as an evacuation center. Walking through streets where skeletons now lay in the rubble, ten-year-old Susumu Desaki found his whole house a heap of ashes. Black bits of his skates and tricycle lay in the debris. Susumu hoped to find his mother and baby sister at the Drill Ground, among the injured soldiers and dead horses. When he found her, his mother's face was so puffy she could not speak. She was holding the baby, who soon died. It was Susumi's job to take his sister's body to an open-air emergency crematorium where the dead were being burned. Each day, he put coconut oil on his mother's burns and washed and changed her dressings, made from strips of clothing. They ate rotten sweet potatoes, then potato leaves, in order to live.[10]

Masayukaai Hayashide, age ten, had been evacuated from the city along with many other children. The day after the bombing, she, too, went looking for her family. With her grandmother, she found them. Her father was not badly hurt, but her mother was burned all over. Her brother and sister had already died. "Mother was completely bedridden," Masayukaai later wrote. "The hair of her head had almost all fallen out, her chest was festering, and from the two-inch hole in her back a lot of maggots were crawling in and out. The place was full of flies and mosquitoes and fleas, and an awfully bad smell hung over everything. . . . All night long she was having trouble breathing. . . . She took one deep breath and did not breathe any more after that."[11]

There was little help for survivors. Like other buildings, hospitals had been destroyed by the bomb, and most of the city's doctors and nurses had died; others were injured. Relief workers came from outside Hiroshima, but they could not keep up with the demand for care, water, and food. Workers passed out rice, biscuits, and cold balls of cooked rice.

Some people were too nauseated to eat, or their mouths were so damaged and sore they could not chew or swallow. They lay in relief shelters surrounded by the smells of human excrement, blood, and vomit. Corpses were everywhere, and there were not enough people to carry away the bodies.

The relief workers did not have enough medicine or oil to rub on burns. Medicine bottles had been broken, spilled, or lost in the explosions and fires. Bandages were scarce. Some people heard that using the ashes of dead relatives on burn victims would soothe their wounds. People used what they had, including machine oil or sliced cucumbers.

Despite the terrible conditions, people showed courage and kindness toward fellow victims. Those in pain did not scream or try to push others aside so they could get help sooner. People helped others who were more seriously hurt. Some risked their lives to rescue trapped people. Those who were uninjured gave first aid.

At the Red Cross Hospital, still partially standing, the lines of people waiting for care grew. Patients crowded every room, and waited on the floors and stairs and in the halls and laboratories. Those who were strong enough tried to help others stand up. About 10,000 people sought care at the hospital, which had only 600 beds, all of them full on the day of the bombing. Makeshift hospitals were set up in schools and in tents erected along the rivers.

Some survivors lay sleeping or unconscious for days. Those who survived usually had some family members who could take care of them. The immediate effects of the bomb had been devastating. As the days went by, it seemed that bomb victims were coming down with other strange symptoms as well. They had diarrhea and strange purple splotches on their skin, and their hair was falling out. Nobody seemed to know what to do for them.

In a relief shelter, young Haruko Okidoi lay on the ground, in terrible pain, her eyes blinded from embedded bits of glass. Sitting with her, her elderly grandmother said: "Can anyone tell me why we got into this war? Our country has been destroyed. Hiroshima has vanished forever. All we can do is pray."[12]

CHAPTER SEVEN: AFTER THE BOMB

The Potsdam Declaration, signed by the Allied leaders, had insisted that Japan surrender or face "utter destruction." At that time, the Japanese did not know about the atomic bomb. Now the people of Hiroshima were suffering the effects of its destructive power.

Iida Momo was a college student in Tokyo who had been relieved not to pass his army physical. Although the Japanese people still had not been told everything about Hiroshima, he later said, "In our house we understood right away that it was an atomic bomb, partly because there had been occasional reports about nuclear research in Japan . . . and partly because my father was in any case interested in that sort of thing. I remember him explaining to us earnestly that with nuclear power, a bomb the size of a matchbox could burn up the whole of the world."[1]

After the bombing, President Truman issued a statement:

> We shall destroy their docks, their factories, and their communications. Let there be no mistake; we shall completely destroy Japan's power to make war. It was to spare the Japanese people from utter destruction that the ultimatum of July 26 was issued at Potsdam. Their leaders promptly rejected that ultimatum. If they do not now accept our terms, they may expect a rain of ruin from the air, the like of which has never been seen on this earth.[2]

The Japanese government discussed what they should do. Foreign Minister Shigenori Tojo, Prime Minister Kantaro Suzuki, and some others wanted to surrender, as did Emperor Hirohito. Some military leaders insisted on continuing the war. Japan received another blow on August 8 when Russia announced it would join the war against Japan.

Iida Momo visited his army friends during those August days. He later recalled, "I knew that in the army it was difficult for them to discover what was really going on." Knowing Russia had declared war, he told his friend Ota: "The war can't possibly go on for more than another week, so keep going, and take care of yourself. If they order you to do anything stupid, don't do it. Whatever happens, don't

The Nagasaki explosion

go and die now. If we survive this war, when it's over, it's going to be our generation's turn, and we're going to do things differently, aren't we?"[3]

Under great tension, the Supreme War Council was again meeting in Tokyo to discuss possible surrender, when a second atomic weapon hit Nagasaki. This bomb was made with plutonium, like the one tested at Alamogordo, New Mexico. As had happened in Hiroshima, the city was devastated. There were eventually about 70,000 dead and 30,000 others wounded, most of them civilians. In a bizarre twist of fate, a kite maker named Shigeyoshi Morimoto experienced both bombings. In Hiroshima on business on August 6, Morimoto had survived and was returning home to Nagasaki on August 9 when the atomic bomb hit that city. Seeing a blue-white flash of light, Morimoto pushed his wife and baby son into the cellar, hurrying in after them. They survived, Morimoto for an incredible second time.

World reactions to the bombings were mixed, with some world leaders condemning them as barbarous and unnecessary. The Vatican spokesman for Roman Catholic officials called the bomb "catastrophic."[4]

To critics, President Truman replied: "I realize the tragic significance of the atomic bomb. Having found the bomb, we have used it . . . against those who attacked us without warning at Pearl Harbor, against those who have starved and beaten and executed American prisoners of war, against those who have abandoned all pretense of obeying international laws of warfare. We have used it in order to shorten the agony of young Americans."[5]

By now, Emperor Hirohito had decided to defy ancient tradition and tell the cabinet to surrender. Speaking of the "bloodshed and cruelty" of the war, the emperor said, "The time has come when we must bear the unbearable."[6] Hirohito offered to accept the end of imperial rule, if the Allies insisted, and even to take full responsibility for the war, in order to stop the suffering. His words, spoken with some tears, resulted in a vote to end the war.

On August 10, one day after Nagasaki, the government sent word via Switzerland and Sweden, which were neutral countries, to the United States, Great Britain, China, and the Soviet Union. The Japanese emperor wished to restore peace and put an end to the agony of his people; he would accept the Potsdam terms.

By August 14, the Allies responded. Plans were made for the demilitarization of Japan and the setting up of an occupation directed by Supreme Commander for the Allied Forces General Douglas MacArthur. U.S. Air Force Superfortress planes dropped leaflets on Tokyo announcing that the nation had surrendered.

Emperor Hirohito recorded a speech for the people on black record discs that were hidden overnight in a safe. Even at this time, some militarists in the government did not want to give up. They tried to find and steal the discs, then killed General Mori and his aide. Fearing for his life, Prime Minister Suzuki fled to safety. General Korechika Anami killed himself in a ritual suicide.

The Japanese heard Hirohito's speech over the radio on August 15, the first time most of them had heard his high-pitched voice. He told his people that because of the bomb, "Should we continue to fight, it would not only result in an ultimate collapse and obliteration of the Japanese nation, but also it would lead to total extinction of human civilization."[7]

As a cease-fire took effect, there was great rejoicing in the Allied nations. Crowds gathered in cities for public celebrations.

Reactions in Japan ranged from relief to anger to sorrow. Never in 2,600 years had Japan suffered a military defeat. Some people cried. Crowds gathered in front of the Imperial Palace.

Saito Mutsuo, an army pilot who was assigned to the suicide squad near the end of the war, later said: "I didn't want Japan to surrender, even though I knew that it would save my life. I suppose that was just the way I had been educated—I believed that we had to fight and never admit defeat, but I thought also that this would be the end of Japan as a nation. The government made a lot of propaganda in those last few months about what would happen if the Americans came."[8]

And what of the response in Hiroshima, where much suffering was still going on? Philip Morrison, a physicist on the Manhattan Project, had gone to Hiroshima after the bombing. He found what he called "one enormous, flat rust-red scar, and no green or gray, because there were no roofs or vegetation left."[9] Some victims told Morrison that the bombing had made it possible for Japan to surrender with honor. Most were now concerned with whether Hiroshima could be made habitable again.

Conditions in the city were growing worse. Takako Okimoto, a seven-year-old at the time, had lost both parents and her two brothers and two sisters. She later wrote, "On the 15th of August, Japan finally became a defeated country. Many beggars appeared in front of the station, and thieves and armed bandits have turned up one after the other, and it has become a world where you aren't safe for a minute."[10]

Japan was a country of disorder, hunger, black markets, and health problems in the fall of 1945. Formal surrender papers between Japan and the Allies were signed on September 2, in Tokyo Bay aboard the U.S.S. *Missouri*. Japan-

Japanese delegates surrender to General Douglas MacArthur (far right) aboard the Missouri.

ese armed forces still in China surrendered to Chiang Kai-shek. Those in northern Korea and Manchuria surrendered to the commander of the forces of the Soviet Union. Although all the Allies were named as occupation forces, only the United States had the resources needed to carry out this task in Japan.

Half of Japan's cities were destroyed. Nearly 3 million Japanese had died, including 800,000 civilians. About 70 million people, as well as the 6 million returning soldiers and civilians from the conquered territories, needed housing and food. Often, families moved in together for shelter, but only farmers had enough food. City dwellers went to farms trying to find food. Japanese money was worth only about one-hundredth of its value before the war, so people gave up treasured possessions—gold, jewelry, silk kimonos, radios—for rice, onions, white potatoes, sweet potatoes, or peas. Vegetable peels, stems, and leaves were saved for soup.

People in Hiroshima made dumplings from horseweed grass mixed with flour made from ground-up acorns. They could be seen pulling carts down the roads. Their clothing was ragged, and many had no shoes. There were no phones or electricity, and the people especially missed their radios.

The Allies had concluded that the harsh treatment and the way the occupation of Germany was conducted after World War I had contributed to the rise of Nazism and World War II. Their goal was to help Japan rebuild, with a stable government and economy. While politicians had

A boy receives cans of food from American servicemen on the Japanese island of Okinawa.

once told Americans to fight the enemy, now they talked about helping Japan. To ease people's fears, General MacArthur told the troops stationed in Japan to be courteous, even to the point of giving up their streetcar seats to elderly women. He set strict rules of conduct. The occupation forces brought food for themselves and the Japanese. U.S. marines made friends, often first with children to whom they gave chocolate bars.

Then the building began. Bombs had destroyed about 30 percent of people's homes, and three-fourths of Japan's industries were not operating. Transportation and communication systems were in bad condition. Seeing that the Americans intended to help them, the Japanese began working hard to repair their cities and towns.

Hiroshima and Nagasaki had the worst damage. Some people in Hiroshima had already erected wooden shacks or huts where their homes had once stood. The city government erected 400 one-family barracks-style homes. Recovering citizens got jobs from the Allies rebuilding and clearing the streets. They began repairing utilities and streetcars.

Schools were held outdoors in good weather. Japanese teachers used revised history books, explaining that their ancestors had been hunting peoples, rather than gods. The emperor announced to the people that he was not a god but a human.

The survivors of the bomb faced many losses and problems. They lived with disfigurement, pain, weakness, recurrent illness, and fear about their futures. Their possessions and homes were gone, and being often sick, they had trouble earning money.

Many bomb victims had large keloid scars—patches of thick, rubbery skin, red in color—where they had suffered burns. These crablike growths embarrassed them and led many to stay at home, rather than be stared at or teased. Scarred children were often taunted by their peers. Eleven-year-old Etsuko Fujioka was called "A-Bomb Scar-face" at school and in the streets. She said, "At the thought of the future I feel afraid to go on living."[11]

In many homes, people hid their mirrors so that burn victims would not realize how they looked. Shigeko had been 13, working in the streets when the bomb fell. She did not know how scarred her face was until she saw her reflection in a piece of glass one day. She later said, "I couldn't believe it was my face. . . . I felt shock, like when someone drops ice-cold water down your back. . . . My face like *this?* I didn't cry out or scream, no noise, but the tears ran like hot water, burning all down my face."[12]

When Shigeko went outside, people called out, "Pikadon, there goes Pikadon." (*Pikadon* was the word that had been given to the atomic bomb, *pika* meaning "flash" and *don*, "a loud noise.") Some survivors thought they were ostracized partly because their scars reminded people of the war and Japan's defeat. They also knew that in some cases their appearance, with features crooked or missing and masses of lumpy, discolored skin, was shocking to people.

Bomb survivors became known as *hibakusha*— "explosion-affected people"—and it became clear that they had many unpredictable health problems. One of these was a distressing set of symptoms known as radiation sickness. The radiation emitted from the bomb had affected the cells of their blood and other body organs. A number of the *hibakusha* lost their hair. Survivors began to fear seeing hairs on their combs, as the radiation sickness led to death in many cases. People with no visible injuries would suddenly become weak, tired, or nauseated, with diarrhea and an outbreak of strange red or purple blotches on their skin. Nobody knew what treatment would truly help them. Some died, while others recovered.

Some women were pregnant at the time of the bombing. When the babies were born, some had physical abnormalities, such as heads smaller than normal. There was a higher-than-normal incidence of mental and physical retardation among these babies. In the 1960s, it was found that some bomb survivors had developed chromosomal damage or abnormalities (changes in the cells' DNA, the substance that controls the passing of traits from parent to offspring) from the invisible radiation that penetrated their body cells.

A disproportionate number of survivors also came down with diseases such as cancers of the blood, thyroid, breast, uterus, and other organs; severe anemia; and other illnesses of the heart, kidneys, glands, skin, and eyes. The process of aging seemed to be greatly speeded up in the *hibakusha*.

As people around the world saw pictures of Hiroshima and Nagasaki and heard about their ordeals in the months that followed the bombings, there was even more controversy over the use of atomic bombs during the war. J. Robert Oppenheimer expressed great surprise at the number of deaths caused by the bombing. He said that the scientists had anticipated more people would seek safety in air-raid shelters when the bombs exploded. The scientists also had not known for sure what effects the radiation from the bombs would cause. Some of the scientists at Los Alamos became distraught when they saw pictures of bomb victims.

Some people in Hiroshima were fatalistic about the bomb. Author John Hersey quoted some as saying, *"Shikata ga nai,"* which means something like, "It can't be helped— oh, well, too bad." Father Kleinsorge, a Jesuit priest from Germany who survived the bombing, said, *"Da ist nichts zu machen*—There is nothing to be done about it."[13] Some Japanese were bitter and enraged at the use of the atomic bomb and hated Americans because of it, saying those who authorized its use should be tried as war criminals.

Other Japanese said that in taking part in the idea of a total war, all the countries had opened themselves to the use of any weapons that would defeat the opponent, even if they were used on civilians. They contended that Japan and Germany would surely have used the atomic bomb if they had developed it first. Many Japanese became less bitter during the occupation. The Americans did not enslave or hurt the people, as they had feared. A number of people were pleased to have a new, democratic form of government.

In the spring of 1946, cabbage, potatoes, tomatoes, and wheat planted earlier in the year began to sprout from the earth in Hiroshima. When a group of thin, blackened cherry trees began to blossom that spring, it was taken as a sign of hope. During the winter, there had been rumors that nothing would ever again grow in the city. People came from all over the city to gaze at the flowering trees.

Despite these signs of hope and life, the hardships and pain of the A-bomb survivors went on. Shintaro Fukuhara, in fourth grade at the time the bomb fell, later wrote simply, "The countless miserable things that happened at that time are quite beyond my pen and my tongue."[14]

The Industry Promotion Hall stands as a reminder of the horrors of the Hiroshima and Nagasaki bombings.

CHAPTER EIGHT: HIROSHIMA TODAY

When Hiroshima was being rebuilt after the war, there was much debate about what to do with the Industry Promotion Hall. The bomb had gutted that once fine building, leaving behind an empty shell and the dome. Should it be reconstructed—torn down and replaced—or left standing as a reminder of the bomb? In the end, it was left untouched. People referred to it as the A-Bomb Dome, and visitors stopped to stare at it. The Dome showed the dual nature of Hiroshima, looking forward on one hand but mindful of the tragic events of the past.

Visitors to Hiroshima are often amazed at how well the city looks today, with few obvious signs that it was once obliterated by an atomic blast. Here is a city of wide roads, modern hotels, tall office buildings, housing complexes, and shopping centers. There are auto plants, factories, and shipyards. A new Aioi Bridge stretches across the Ota River. People sit at ice-cream parlors or at riverside restaurants where they enjoy oysters and other seafood and sip sake. The ancient wooden castle was rebuilt of concrete and is now a museum. Many people wear Western-style T-shirts and denim jeans. The city sponsors a baseball team, the Hiroshima Carps.

Japan as a whole has likewise recovered and become a respected nation. The Japanese constitution, developed after the war, promoted democracy and human rights and renounced war. Formerly its chief enemy, the United States spent about a half billion dollars a year to feed people and to rebuild Japan during the occupation. Today, Japan is an economic superpower, with successful industries—electronic, petrochemical, auto, computer, microelectronic, camera, textile, medical, paper, and fishing. It is a leading exporter of VCRs, televisions, radios, stereo equipment, cameras, and steel.

The United States and democratic Japan became allies after the war. During the Korean War (1950–1953), Japan was a base for the United Nations and U.S. military forces that were fighting in Korea. These troops used Japan's harbors and airfields, as well as its hospitals. During these years, the occupation troops were gradually withdrawn. The two nations signed a mutual security pact in 1951, and in 1952, the occupation was declared officially over.

However, for the 90,000 survivors of Hiroshima, the effects of the August 6 bombing went on. In his award-winning 1946 book *Hiroshima,* author John Hersey wrote in detail about six survivors, whom he interviewed after the bombing. When he found them again in the following years, Hersey reported they were still suffering because of the bomb. One was crippled; another was extremely poor. Two men had ongoing illnesses and could not work as before. A doctor had lost the hospital he spent years building up.

The story of Mrs. Nakamura, the tailor's widow who survived with her three younger children, shows the plight of many *hibakusha*. Mrs. Nakamura was combing her hair two weeks after the bombing when she noticed clumps of it on her comb. She became weak and tired, as did her youngest daughter, Myeko. They were both suffering from radiation sickness.

Within the next year, the family became destitute. Mrs. Nakamura rescued and repaired the sewing machine she had placed in the water tank during the bombing. By sewing and doing laundry and cleaning for people, she earned just about enough for food. She would work three days, then have to rest for two.

Soon she was sick again, with a sore, swollen abdomen and diarrhea. She had intestinal parasites, common in those days. To pay for treatment, she had to sell her sewing machine—something Mrs. Nakamura later called the lowest point in her life. After recovering, she earned 50 cents a day selling bread for a baker, but still had to rest often. Then she sold fish door-to-door from a pushcart, buying sardines from fishermen at a river near the Ota. A couple of years later, she earned $20 a month collecting money for the city's newspaper, which most citizens read.

The family had some assistance in 1951. An American Quaker professor, Dr. Floyd Schmoe, organized a home-building project called Peace Houses. Schmoe's group, made up of himself, his wife, and people from different countries, built houses that the Japanese government rented for one dollar a month. Mrs. Nakamura was able to rent one of these homes and used her old hut as a stand to sell roasted sweet potatoes and rice cakes to schoolchildren. Like many *hibakusha,* she found that most employers did not want to hire her, for fear she would often be sick. (Survivors also feared being rejected as marriage partners, and some moved to new places where they did not tell people about their past.) Finally, Mrs. Nakamura got a job at a factory, where she started at a salary of 50 cents a day. She made friends and developed more interest in life.

A group of people who suffered special hardships were those who had been badly scarred at a young age. School-girls who had been clearing fire lanes on the day of the bombing were near the point where the bomb exploded. They were left with disfigured faces, bodies, and limbs. Some had lost fingers or the use of their arms and legs. Knowing they were no longer considered "marriageable," and embar-rassed by the stares and rude comments of others, some of these girls isolated themselves at home.

Another survivor, the Reverend Kyoshi Tanimoto,

started a Society of Keloid Girls, where these young women found mutual support and did sewing and other projects. Tanimoto asked the government to pay for plastic surgery to improve the girls' health and appearance, but he was unsuccessful. A woman journalist from Tokyo helped to raise money so that some of the girls could have surgery in Tokyo, then in Osaka. These young women became known as A-Bomb Maidens—*Genbaku Otome*—or Hiroshima Maidens.

In 1955, 25 of the Maidens were flown to the United States to get free medical treatment in American hospitals, where plastic surgery techniques were more advanced. While in treatment, the Maidens lived for a year with Quaker families in the New York City area. Norman Cousins, editor in chief of the *Saturday Review,* had visited Hiroshima and spearheaded this project, as well as a fund-raising project for orphans. He continued to keep in touch with and help Maidens and other people in Hiroshima and set up the Hiroshima Peace Center Foundation in New York City.

By the 1950s, the Japanese government also had begun to respond more to the problems of Hiroshima survivors. The A-Bomb Hospital, with 170 beds, was completed in 1956. Since that time, these beds have always been filled with *hibakusha* patients. To be officially classified as a bomb victim, a person must either have lived within the city limits of Hiroshima on August 6, been born to a mother who lived there at that time, or come to the city to see family members or to help with the relief efforts within two weeks after the bombing.

In 1957, the Japanese Diet also passed the A-Bomb Victims Medical Care Law. Besides health coupon books for medical care, it entitled people to monthly allowances, which helped those with health problems and special needs.

Because they had actually experienced the bomb, people in Japan understood better than most others its disastrous consequences. Yet public awareness was increasing throughout the world. Photographs of Hiroshima and stories about the ongoing suffering there prompted people in other countries to express concern about how to control nuclear weapons and prevent future wars.

Even before the first bombs were completed, scientists and government leaders in the United States had begun discussing the implications for the future. They feared that more nations would eventually build atomic weapons, a fear that was quickly realized in 1949, when the Soviet Union tested an atomic bomb.

Unknown to the other Allies, the Soviet Union had gained a great deal of technical information from spies working on the Manhattan Project. President Truman later recalled that he had had a hint of this knowledge at the 1945 Potsdam Conference. At that time, he had told Stalin that the United States "had a new weapon of unusual destructive force." Stalin had not asked questions or shown any special interest.[1] Due mainly to an Austrian-born spy who came to Los Alamos with the British scientists, Stalin knew about the bomb in 1945. Soviet scientists had begun making atomic weapons. Thus the Russians felt more free to sweep across Eastern Europe, setting up Soviet-controlled governments after the war, because they, too, had weapons of "unusual destructive force."

Truman asked the U.S. Congress to establish an Atomic Energy Commission to control the production and use of atomic power. In November 1945, he joined the leaders of Great Britain and Canada in a proclamation that said: "Faced with the terrible realities of the application of science to destruction, every nation will realize more urgently than before the overwhelming need to maintain the rule of law among nations and to banish the scourge of war from the earth."[2] Writing in 1947 about the decision to use the bomb, Secretary of War Henry L. Stimson said, "In this last great action of the Second World War we were given final proof that war is death. War in the twentieth century has grown steadily more barbarous, more destructive, more debased in all its aspects. . . . The bombs dropped on Hiroshima and Nagasaki ended a war. They also made it wholly clear that we must never have another war. . . . There is no other choice."[3]

People involved in the war and in making the atomic bomb echoed these thoughts. After the war, J. Robert Oppenheimer spoke out fervently for world peace. He said: "The peoples of the world must unite or perish. This war, that has ravaged so much of the earth, has written these words. The atomic bomb has spelled them out for all men to understand."[4] Oppenheimer and others advocated international control and treaties. They hoped the newly created United Nations Atomic Energy Commission would lead this effort.

But the United States and the Soviet Union, emerging as world superpowers after World War II, distrusted each other. Both went on to develop new and more destructive weapons. In the 1950s, Edward Teller finished developing a hydrogen bomb, called the "super," which was far more powerful than the bombs of 1945. In the following decades, both sides built new and more destructive weapons, such as intercontinental ballistic missiles (ICBMs), which carried bombs across continents with more than 500 times more force than the Hiroshima bomb, and cruise missiles, which can be launched from a distance of about 1,500 miles (2,415 kilometers), while those fired from submarines in World War II went about 6 miles (9.6 kilometers). Along with these weapons, countries developed early warning radar systems to protect them from attacks.

In 1963, the United States and Soviet Union signed the first nuclear arms control treaty. In this partial Nuclear Test-Ban Treaty, they agreed not to test nuclear weapons in space or in the seas. Limits also were placed on underground testing to reduce the polluting effects of radioactive fallout. Five years later came the Non-Proliferation treaty, an

In 1957, a woman signs a petition asking for an end to nuclear testing.

attempt to prevent more countries from making nuclear weapons if they did not have them already. Besides the United States, the Soviet Union, France, and Britain, 124 nonnuclear countries also signed this 1968 treaty. These nations were helped to develop nuclear power plants for peacetime electrical energy. Yet other countries—Israel, Pakistan, India, and South Africa—went on to develop nuclear weapons.

Reducing the rate of weapons production became the next step. In 1972, the United States and the Soviet Union, with about 15,000 weapons apiece, agreed to slow down the arms race. The Strategic Arms Limitation Talks (SALT) forbid more than a set number of long-range ground and seaborne missiles. The year 1989 finally brought an agreement to reduce the number of existing weapons, of which there were 50,000. In the meantime, by 1990, a total of 111 countries had signed the 1963 partial Nuclear Test-Ban Treaty.

Through these decades of international tension and negotiations, people who protested the arms buildup, joined "Ban the Bomb" demonstrations, or spoke up for the cause of peace often invoked the memory of Hiroshima. The city itself has become a world peace center. The wish that their experience might help humankind was expressed by a survivor and peace activist, the Reverend Kyoshi Tanimoto, in a speech he made early in 1949, more than 40 years ago:

> The people of Hiroshima . . . have accepted
> as a compelling responsibility their mission
> to help in preventing further similar destruc-
> tion anywhere in the world. . . . [They]
> earnestly desire that out of their experience
> there may develop some permanent contri-
> bution to the cause of world peace. Towards
> this end, we propose the establishment of a

World Peace Center, international and non-
sectarian, which will serve as a laboratory of
research and planning for peace education
throughout the world.[5]

That year, the Japanese Diet declared Hiroshima a
Peace Memorial City. Part of the city was devoted to a park
that holds memorials for bomb victims and pleas for a peace-
ful world. It is situated on the hypocenter of the explosion.
Besides the Atomic Dome, there is a cenotaph, built like
an ancient clay house, where the names of everyone who
died as a result of the bomb have been inscribed. Walking
along the grassy pathways, people stop to place flowers
there. It is believed that the souls of the departed live in
this place. An inscription near their names says, "Rest in
peace. The mistake will not be repeated."

There also is a Memorial Mound for the Unknown
Dead, containing a vault with the ashes of unidentified victims. A Children's Monument was built in 1958 in honor
of Sadako Sasaki. Only two years old in 1945, Sadako died
at age 12 from leukemia, thought to have been caused by
radiation. According to tradition, a person who folds a thousand paper cranes is kept safe from illness. Sadako folded
cranes in the hospital and had reached a total of 964 before
she died in 1955.

At the annual memorial ceremonies held on August 6,
people remember loved ones who died from "The Flash" by

Thousands of paper lanterns inscribed with the names of bomb victims float down Hiroshima's Motoyasu River in the shadow of the A-bomb Dome on August 6, 1985, in a memorial ceremony.

writing their names on lanterns. The lanterns are then lit and set to float out to sea on one of the city's seven rivers.

Inside the Peace Memorial Museum are photographs of the bombing and a collection of objects that were bent, melted, and twisted almost beyond recognition. Clumps of human hair and black fingernails are among the grisly reminders of that August day. There are slabs of concrete where eerie shadows of incinerated people were left imprinted on the sides of bridges and walls around the city. There is a watch someone dropped in the sand that day; its hands are stopped at exactly 8:16 A.M.

"We cannot escape history," Abraham Lincoln once said. The history of this first atomic bomb is a story of momentous scientific discoveries, wartime politics, and immeasurable suffering. Since that time, more atomic weapons have been built, tested, and set in place, able to destroy whole nations at the push of a button. Because human beings now have the means to destroy all life on earth, the world has never been the same. For that reason, it has been said that all of us, struggling to live with this ominous knowledge, are in a sense "survivors" of Hiroshima.

* * *

SOURCE NOTES

Prologue
1. John Costello, *The Pacific War* (New York: Rawson, Wade, 1981), p. 591.
2. Quoted in Dan Kurzman, *Day of the Bomb: Countdown to Hiroshima* (New York: McGraw-Hill, 1986), p. 265.
3. Ibid.

Chapter One
1. Anne Chisholm, *Faces of Hiroshima* (London: Jonathan Cape, 1985), p. 17.
2. From a memorandum by the U.S. assistant military attaché in Japan, reprinted in *Foreign Relations in the United States 1932* (Washington: U.S. Dept. of State, 1948), p. 713; quoted in Tessa Morris-Suzuki, *SHOWA* (New York: Schocken, 1985), p. 21.
3. Morris-Suzuki, p. 22.
4. Quoted in Chisholm, p. 16.

Chapter Two
1. Morris-Suzuki, p. 41.
2. John R. Roberson, *Japan: From Shogun to SONY: 1543 to 1984* (New York: Atheneum, 1985), p. 137.
3. Joseph C. Grew, *The Turbulent Era: A Diplomatic Record of Forty Years, Vol. II* (Boston: Houghton Mifflin, 1952), p. 359.
4. Thomas B. Allen, "Pearl Harbor: A Return to the Day of Infamy," *National Geographic*, December 1991, pp. 62–63.
5. Ibid., p. 63.

6. John Toland, *The Rising Sun* (New York: Random House, 1970), p. 283.
7. Chisholm, p. 16.
8. Toland, p. 287.
9. Kurzman, p. 292.
10. Morris-Suzuki, p. 62.
11. Eric Larrabee, *Franklin Delano Roosevelt: His Lieutenants and Their War* (New York: Harper and Row, 1987), p. 646.

Chapter Three
1. Kurzman, pp. 27–28.
2. James M. Burns, *Roosevelt: The Soldier of Freedom* (New York: Harcourt, Brace, 1970), p. 250; Larrabee, p. 645.
3. Kurzman, p. 21.
4. Lansing Lamont, *Day of Trinity* (New York: Atheneum, 1965), p. 30.
5. Arthur H. Compton, *Atomic Quest* (New York: Oxford, 1956), p. 64.
6. Compton, p. 117.
7. Lamont, p. 73.

Chapter Four
1. Jean Darby, *Douglas MacArthur* (Minneapolis: Lerner, 1989), p. 77.
2. Hiroko Nakamoto and M. M. Pace, *My Japan: 1930–51* (New York: McGraw-Hill, 1970); quoted in Chisholm, p. 20.
3. Pacific War Research Society, *The Day Man Lost* (Tokyo: Kodansha International, 1981), p. 137.
4. Len Giovannitti and Fred Freed, *The Decision to Drop the Bomb* (New York: Coward-McCann, 1965), p. 130.
5. Quoted in Costello, p. 189.

Chapter Five
1. Harry S Truman, *Memoirs by Harry S Truman. Vol. I: Year of Decisions* (Garden City, New York: Doubleday, 1955), p. 10.
2. Quoted in Keith Wheeler, *The Fall of Japan* (New York: Time-Life, 1983), p. 60.
3. Leslie R. Groves, *Now It Can Be Told* (New York: Da Capo, 1962); quoted in Wheeler, p. 60.
4. U.S. Atomic Energy Commission, Transcript of Hearing before Personnel Security Board, In the Matter of J. Robert Oppenheimer, Washington, D.C., 1954, p. 34; quoted in Herbert Feis, *The Atomic Bomb and the End of World War II* (Princeton, New Jersey: Princeton University Press, 1966), p. 55.
5. Truman, pp. 419–420.
6. Quoted in Giovannitti and Freed, p. 197.
7. Truman, p. 415.
8. Roberson, p. 154.
9. Quoted in Giovannitti and Freed, pp. 38–39.
10. Nakamoto and Pace, *My Japan*, quoted in Chisholm, pp. 21–22.

Chapter Six
1. Quoted in Gordon Thomas and Max Morgan Witts, *Enola Gay* (New York: Stein and Day, 1977), p. 94.
2. Roger Rosenblatt, *Witness: The World Since Hiroshima* (Boston: Little, Brown, 1985), p. 19.
3. John Hersey, *Hiroshima* (New York: Knopf, 1988), p. 116.
4. Peter Wydén, *Day One: Before Hiroshima and After* (New York: Simon and Schuster, 1984), p. 255.
5. Ibid., pp. 259–260.
6. Ibid., p. 261.
7. Rosenblatt, pp. 10–17.

8. Hersey, p. 27.
9. Lester Brooks, *Behind Japan's Surrender* (New York: McGraw-Hill, 1968), p. 166.
10. Wyden, pp. 271–272.
11. Arata Osada, *Children of the A-Bomb* (New York: Putnam, 1963), p. 155.
12. Pacific War Research Society, p. 287.

Chapter Seven
1. Morris-Suzuki, p. 182.
2. Truman, p. 422.
3. Morris-Suzuki, pp. 182–183.
4. Quoted in Thomas and Witts, p. 273.
5. Feis, p. 130.
6. Costello, p. 593.
7. Roberson, pp. 160–161.
8. Morris-Suzuki, p. 140.
9. Daniel Lang, *From Hiroshima to the Moon* (New York: Simon and Schuster, 1959), p. 43.
10. Osada, p. 100.
11. Ibid., p. 174.
12. Chisholm, p. 33.
13. Hersey, p. 17.
14. Osada, p. 152.

Chapter Eight
1. Truman, p. 416.
2. Feis, p. 175.
3. Henry L. Stimson, "The Decision to Use the Atomic Bomb," in Richard N. Current et al., *Words That Made American History* (Boston: Little, Brown, 1972), p. 474.
4. Peter Goodchild, *J. Robert Oppenheimer: Shatterer of Worlds* (New York: Fromm International, 1985), p. 172.
5. Hersey, pp. 177–178.

FOR FURTHER READING

Amrine, Michael. *The Great Decision*. New York: Putnam, 1959.

Asahi, Shimbun. *A-Bomb*. Hiroshima, Japan: Hiroshima Peace Culture Center, 1972.

Barker, Rodney. *The Hiroshima Maidens*. New York: Viking, 1985.

Batschelder, Robert C. *The Irreversible Decision*. Boston: Houghton Mifflin, 1961.

Beasley, W. G. *The Modern History of Japan*. New York: Praeger, 1963.

Bernstein, Barton J. *The Atomic Bomb: The Critical Issues*. Boston: Little, Brown, 1976.

Brooks, Lester. *Behind Japan's Surrender*. New York: McGraw-Hill, 1968.

Burns, James M. *Roosevelt: The Soldier of Freedom*. New York: Harcourt, Brace, 1970.

Chisholm, Anne. *Faces of Hiroshima*. London: Jonathan Cape, 1985.

Compton, Arthur Holly. *Atomic Quest*. New York: Oxford, 1956.

Costello, John. *The Pacific War*. New York: Rawson, Wade, 1981.

Craig, William. *The Fall of Japan*. New York: Dial, 1967.

Darby, Jean. *Douglas MacArthur*. Minneapolis: Lerner, 1989.

Davis, Nuel Pharr. *Lawrence and Oppenheimer*. New York: Simon and Schuster, 1968.

Feis, Herbert. *The Atomic Bomb and the End of World War II*. Princeton, New Jersey: Princeton University Press, 1966.

Fermi, Laura. *Atoms in the Family*. Chicago: University of Chicago Press, 1954.

Giovannitti, Len, and Fred Freed. *The Decision to Drop the Bomb*. New York: Coward-McCann, 1965.

Goodchild, Peter. *J. Robert Oppenheimer: Shatterer of Worlds*. New York: Fromm International, 1985.

Grew, Joseph C. *Ten Years in Japan*. New York: Arno, 1972.

Groeff, Stephan. *Manhattan Project*. Boston: Little, Brown, 1967.

Groves, Leslie R. *Now It Can Be Told*. New York: Da Capo, 1962.

Hachiya, Michihiko. *Hiroshima Diary*. Translated by W. Wells. Chapel Hill, North Carolina: University of North Carolina Press, 1969.

Hersey, John. *Hiroshima*. New York: Knopf, 1988.

Ibuse, Masuji. *Black Rain*. Translated by John Bestor. Tokyo: Kodansha International, 1969.

Jungk, Robert. *Children of the Ashes*. New York: Harcourt, Brace, 1961.

Junod, Marcel. "Visiting Hiroshima, 9 Sept 1945," in *Eyewitness to History*, edited by John Carey, pp. 638–640. Cambridge, Massachusetts: Harvard University Press, 1988.

Kurzman, Dan. *Day of the Bomb: Countdown to Hiroshima*. New York: McGraw-Hill, 1986.

Lamont, Lansing. *Day of Trinity*. New York: Atheneum, 1965.

Lang, Daniel. *From Hiroshima to the Moon*. New York: Simon and Schuster, 1959.

Larrabee, Eric. *Franklin Delano Roosevelt: His Lieutenants and Their War*. New York: Harper and Row, 1987.

Lawson, Don. *The United States in World War II*. New York: Abelard-Schuman, 1963.

Lifton, Betty Jean. *A Place Called Hiroshima*. Tokyo: Kodansha International, 1985.

Lifton, Robert. *Death in Life: Survivors of Hiroshima*. New York: Random House, 1967.

Morris-Suzuki, Tessa. *SHOWA: An Inside History of Hirohito's Japan*. New York: Schocken, 1985.

Nakamoto, Hiroko, and M. M. Pace. *My Japan: 1930–51*. New York: McGraw-Hill, 1970.

Osada, Arata. *Children of the A-Bomb*. Translated by Jean Dan and Ruth Sieben-Morgan. New York: Putnam, 1963.

Osaka, Ichiro. *Hiroshima 1945*. Tokyo: Chuko Shinso, 1975.

Ota, Y. *Shikabane no Machi Town of Corpses*. Tokyo: Kawade Shobo, 1955.

Oughterson, A. W., and S. Warren, eds. *Medical Effects of the Atomic Bomb in Japan*. New York: McGraw-Hill, 1956.

Philbin, Marianne, ed. *The Ribbon: A Celebration of Life*. Asheville, North Carolina: Lark Books, 1985.

Rhodes, Richard. *The Making of the Atomic Bomb*. New York: Simon and Schuster, 1986.

Roberson, John R. *Japan: From Shogun to SONY: 1543 to 1984*. New York: Atheneum, 1985.

Rosenblatt, Roger. *Witness: The World Since Hiroshima*. Boston: Little, Brown, 1985.

Spector, Ronald H. *Eagle Against the Sun: The American War with Japan*. New York: Macmillan, 1985.

Storry, Richard. *A History of Modern Japan*. New York: Penguin, 1960.

Sweeney, James B. *Army Leaders of World War II*. New York: Franklin Watts, 1984.

Takayama, Hitoshi, ed. *Hiroshima in Memoriam and Today*. Hiroshima: Hiroshima Peace Culture Center, 1973.

Teller, Edward, and Allen Brown. *The Legacy of Hiroshima*. Westport, Connecticut: Greenwood, 1962.

Thomas, Gordon, and Max Morgan Witts. *Enola Gay*. New York: Stein and Day, 1977.

Toland, John. *The Rising Sun*. New York: Random House, 1970.

Truman, Harry S. *Memoirs of Harry S Truman. Vol. I: Year of Decisions*. Garden City, New York: Doubleday, 1955.

Trumbull, Robert. *Nine Who Survived Hiroshima and Nagasaki*. New York: Dutton, 1957.

Wheeler, Keith. *The Fall of Japan*. New York: Time-Life, 1983.

Wyden, Peter. *Day One: Before Hiroshima and After*. New York: Simon and Schuster, 1984.

INDEX